MW01290426

Hooked

Tales & Adventures of a

TAILHOOK
WARRIOR

CDR Clayton E. Fisher, USN (Ret)

Outskirts Press, Inc.
Denver, Colorado

Outskirts Press, Inc.
http://www.outskirtspress.com

ISBN PB: 978-1-4327-2279-1
ISBN HB: 978-1-4327-3911-9

Library of Congress Control Number: 2008938460

Outskirts Press and the "OP" logo are trademarks belonging to Outskirts Press, Inc.

PRINTED IN THE UNITED STATES OF AMERICA

TESTIMONIAL

"A stirring tale told by a brave man who served his country long and well. It is told clearly and concisely, with no false heroics and with honesty, warts and all."

Peter C. Smith
Military Historian and British Author

DEDICATION

To:

Annie, who had the strength and courage to marry me during those turbulent times in the early months of WWII — the war that could have ripped our lives apart.

This book is for you.

To:

The Tailhooker pilots and their aircrew men who died during the aircraft carrier battles of Midway, Santa Cruz in 1942 and later during the Korean conflict, 1951/52.

They have missed so much.

ACKNOWLEDGEMENTS

To: My two daughters, Susan "Susie" McClure and Roberta "Bobbie" Dennis, and my five grandchildren, Michael "Mike" Beauchamp, Alison Kobbervig, Evan McClure, Megan "Meggie" McClure and Heather McClure for their continued interest in my book project.

To: Alison and Bobbie who continually encouraged me to write narratives about my combat experiences which enabled me to write my book.

To: Annie, my partner and "buddy" for sixty-seven years, for prodding me to write the book and her helpful suggestions as to its content and grammar.

To: Bobbie for her expertise and creative talents in assisting in the preparation of the book cover, editing the manuscript text and providing liaison with the author and the publisher's representative.

To: Peter C. Smith, prominent British military history author of over 68 published books for his professional advice and personal comments to a "rookie" author.

To: R.G. Smith

As a Douglas Dauntless SBD dive-bomber pilot during the Battle of Midway, I always admired the depictions of the battle by R.G. Smith, a famous painter of naval warfare.

One of his best Midway paintings has a vibrant and dynamic rendering of two SBD dive bombers crossing near the bow of a Japanese aircraft carrier. I knew I wanted to use a modified reproduction of the painting to specifically highlight one of the SBDs for the front cover of this book.

Prior to his painting successes he was employed by Douglass Aircraft and helped to design the SBD Dauntless dive bomber. The SBD dive bombers were responsible for all the direct bomb hits that resulted in the destruction and final sinking of all four Japanese aircraft carriers during the Battle of Midway

R.G. Smith, deceased, and his daughter Mrs. Sharlyn Marsh is now his agent. She graciously granted me permission to reproduce one of his famous Battle of Midway paintings, "SBDs over Akagi," which was used in the cover design for "Hooked."

TABLE OF CONTENTS

Testimonial			iii
Dedication			v
Acknowledgements			vii
Table of Contents			ix
Foreword			xi
Prologue			xiii
Chapter	1	Hooked	1
Chapter	2	Flight Training	9
Chapter	3	Bombing Squadron Eight	25
Chapter	4	Hornet's Shake Down Cruise	35
Chapter	5	Hornet's Deployment to the Pacific Fleet	45
Chapter	6	San Diego and San Francisco	51
Chapter	7	The B-25 Mission to Bomb Tokyo 18 April 1942	55
Chapter	8	Deployment to South Pacific	61
Chapter	9	Return to Pearl Harbor	67
Chapter	10	The Battle of Midway 4 June 1942	73
Chapter	11	The Battle of Midway 5 June 1942	91
Chapter	12	The Battle of Midway 6 June 1942	99
Chapter	13	Pearl Harbor and South Pacific	103
Chapter	14	Battle of Santa Cruz 26 October 1942	111
Chapter	15	USS Solace and Lurliner	127

Chapter	16	Naval Air Station Fort Lauderdale	137
Chapter	17	Lake Michigan - Aircraft Training Carriers	143
Chapter	18	Naval Air Station Vero Beach	151
Chapter	19	Night Fighter Operational Flight Training	165
Chapter	20	Interlude Between WWII and the Korean War	183
Chapter	21	Fighter Squadron Fifty Three	195
Chapter	22	Korean War	201
Chapter	23	Duty on the Beach	227

FOREWORD

During WWII American and Japanese fighter aircraft were deadly predators when they attacked enemy bomber aircraft. In a one-on-one encounter of a fighter and a bomber, the bomber and its crew seldom survived.

PROLOGUE

When I finally leveled off at 300 feet, my gunner yelled, "We got a *Zero* on our tail!" Putting it mildly, it was a horrifying feeling. I couldn't out maneuver the *Zero*. With a *Zero* on its tail, a *SBD* dive bomber has a slight advantage over a single fighter because of the gunner's rapid-firing, twin 30-caliber guns. So I dove closer to the water where the fighter couldn't get in a position below us – a dangerous spot because the gunner couldn't position his guns to bear down on the *Zero*. My gunner, ARM 3/c Ferguson, practically shot off our rudder trying to hit the *Zero*. Both wings were riddled with small jagged holes after being hit with 7.7mm bullets. One bullet passed between my legs, shattering my engine's cylinder temperature gauge.

Finally, the *Zero* fired his 20mm cannons, and a shell exploded in the radio transmitter located behind my armored seat. A radio-frequency manual was blown to bits with confetti flying all over the cockpit. The concussion from the exploding shell inside the confines of the cockpit canopy felt like I had been hit a hard blow on top of my head. Simultaneously, I felt a red-hot burning sensation in my right arm just below my shoulder. Shrapnel fragments flying around in the cockpit had hit my upper right arm just above the elbow. Momentarily stunned, I had lost my vision, but my mind was visualizing the shimmering, wavering faces of my mother and Annie. I didn't want to die, but felt completely helpless. After recovering from the shock of the concussion and as my vision cleared, the *Zero* fighter, with its big red "meatball" insignia, was flying off my right wing, just like a wingman. The pilot was staring at me! When our eyes met, he drifted back behind us. Ferguson had been shot in both thighs with 7.7-mm bullets and a piece of shrapnel had gouged some flesh out of the calf of his right leg. Ferguson managed to reload his jammed guns, in spite of his wounds, and waited for the *Zero* to get into firing range. The *Zero's* pilot evidently felt we were "cold turkey" and moved slowly back into position for the kill. Ferguson fired first and hit the engine of the *Zero*. The *Zero* with its engine smoking, pulled up sharply away from us, and then disappeared. We had miraculously survived; Ferguson had not panicked. He had saved both our lives.

CHAPTER 1
HOOKED

I magine being a four-year old boy in 1923, in a small town in the southern Wisconsin farmlands. On a sunny afternoon, while playing in your own front yard, you hear a distant noise, strange to your ears, which causes you to pause, listen more closely, and look up. A huge – no, gigantic – monster bird was flying directly overhead. I was that four-year old boy, scared and panic stricken. I ran screaming back to our house, smashing my hands into the front screen door. My mother gathered me in her arms and held me until I stopped crying. What spooked me wasn't a huge bird, but a World War I vintage aircraft – to be exact an Army Air Corps two-seater *Curtiss Jenny* biplane. The pilot had zoomed low over our house and town to attract attention, and landed his plane in a cow pasture near Footville. Not missing an opportunity, my father took me to the pasture to see the airplane. He hoisted me in his arms, and I gingerly touched one of the wooden propeller blades, which looked like arms to me. The barnstorming pilot was selling rides, and I couldn't understand why his passengers rode in the front seat, instead of the back seat, like I did in our family's *Model T Ford*.

My next memory of an exciting aviation event was Charles Lindbergh's solo flight in the *Spirit of Saint Louis* from New York to Paris in May 1927. It became a lead story as the news of his success flooded the airways and newspapers. Lindbergh became a national hero, and he sparked an interest in aviation, especially, for many young boys like me. We kids considered Lindbergh to be the greatest pilot on earth! Lindy later became the nickname for Lindbergh and also became a favorite name for many pet dogs. He toured the United

States in the *Spirit of Saint Louis* and landed at our local city airport in 1928. Waiting with anticipation, I finally watched Lindy land his plane — the same plane that had crossed the Atlantic Ocean — and my heart and mind were forever imprinted. Hooked, I wanted to be an aviator!

In 1929, when I was ten, our family moved to Janesville, Wisconsin, where we shared a home with my grandparents to weather out the *Great Depression.* We lived near the county fairgrounds, which included a harness horse-racing track called the *Lexington of the North.* Inside the oval one-mile race track, there was a large green infield with enough space to accommodate the landings and takeoffs of small biplanes. For a young boy who was now addicted to airplanes, it was a dream come true to be living so close to the fairgrounds. During the summer barnstorming pilots used the field and charged a couple bucks a ride. Although, it was during the depression when a couple of bucks was a lot of money, I was able to scrounge up enough to get rides in a variety of planes, sometimes weird-looking ones. Every flight was exciting, especially taking off and landing.

On the Fourth of July, I had the experience of taking a ride in a small twin-engine powered blimp and was lucky enough to be able to sit next to the pilot. The sensation of being in a blimp is similar to floating down a river in a boat. As we quietly glided along with the engines idling, the noisy firecrackers below were an exciting contrast to my airborne experience. As the blimp approached the fairgrounds, for its landing, we happened to pass right over my house. There was my mother looking up, unaware I was looking down at her from my lofty ride in the sky.

Months later at our new city airport I helped a pilot refuel his *Ford Tri-Motor,* all-metal monoplane, and for that small favor, he gave me a free ride. In contrast to the serene blimp ride, I was amazed at how much noise the three engines created in the passenger's cabin. In spite of that drawback, the *Ford Tri-Motor* with its light wicker seats went on to become America's first successful commercial airliner.

In 1930, Howard Hughes produced the movie *Hell's Angels,* which along with *Gone with the Wind,* was one of the two greatest hits of that era. *Hell's Angels* featured stunning aerial footage and realistic dogfights, and the flying scenes captivated me. Coincidentally, a new eighteen year old sultry blonde movie actress named Jean Harlow gained her stardom from this movie. Being eleven years old, Jean Harlow was only of secondary interest to me.

Hell's Angels fired my interest to become a fighter pilot in the Army Air Corps. The Army Air Corps and the Navy had established flight training programs that required two years of college education. Upon completion, flight students were then designated as Aviation Cadets. Marty Lien, a close friend and next-door neighbor, was already in the Naval Aviation Flight Program. Marty had won his gold wings at the Naval Air Station Pensacola, Florida. We corresponded regularly while I was finishing high school, and his descriptive letters about each stage of his flight training and the Navy gold wings printed on his stationary deeply impressed me. After graduation, Marty was assigned to Bombing Squadron Five stationed aboard the *USS Yorktown,* and he was now a dive-bomber pilot. This was the impetus I needed. Now, I wanted to enter the Navy's flight program and become a naval aviator, but I needed two years of college to qualify for the Naval Aviation Flight Program.

After graduating from Janesville High School in 1937, I attended Milton College, a small Seventh Day Adventist college in Milton, Wisconsin. As an engineering student, I completed science classes in calculus, physics and chemistry. In addition, I won two athletic letters in track for running the 440-yard dash and also played football as a running back. The cost for each semester for college tuition, books and living expenses was sixty dollars. Although I had several summer jobs, I still needed additional money to cover all of the expenses.

To supplement my meager income, I enlisted in the Wisconsin National Guard's 32nd Division's Tank Company, located in Janesville, Wisconsin. You had to be eighteen-years old to enlist and sign a three-year enlistment contract. Being only seventeen, I lied about my age, signed the contract and then told my parents. They were upset, but didn't divulge my true age which would have terminated

3

my contract. I was a lowly private earning one dollar per week, but in my second year I was promoted to corporal in the Tank Company earning a dollar fifty for drilling two nights a week at the local Janesville armory. With two summer training encampments at Camp Douglas, Wisconsin, I was now on my way to a military career.

The training was intensive, and I learned to fire the standard issue Army Colt 45-caliber pistol and the 30-caliber light cavalry machine gun. The tank company had only two modern light tanks, but us lowly types never trained in them. As an eighteen-year-old corporal, I became the leader of an eight-man squad of men all older than me. It took a while, but I gained the men's respect, and the age difference never became a problem.

After completing two years of college at Milton, I applied for the Naval Aviation Flight Program and was upset when informed by letter that Milton College was not an approved school. Dejected, I rationalized that wanting to become a naval aviator was probably as much of a reality as becoming a fireman or policeman. However, after more soul searching, I made the decision to transfer to the University of Wisconsin for my junior year. This decision may have saved my life. While attending the university, I couldn't attend the weekly drills in the National Guard, so I was able to terminate my three-year enlistment contract after two and one-half years and was honorably discharged. Shortly after I was discharged, the Tank Company was nationalized — under federal control — then sent to Fort Knox, Tennessee and assigned to the 192nd Tank Battalion. The battalion was then ordered to the Philippines and arrived there in November 1941. After the attack on Pearl Harbor, 7 December 1941, President Roosevelt declared war with the Japanese. The Tank Company of 130 officers and men were captured in the Philippines. Only eight men survived.

HOOKED

Private Fisher - Camp Douglas, Wisconsin, 1938

At the University of Wisconsin, I supported myself by working a part-time job at the university for fifty cents an hour. As an engineering student, I made the mistake of taking too many classes and laboratory units each semester. Because of the overload, I became mentally and physically exhausted and very discouraged. As we were approaching the end of the last semester, my roommate and I were running out of food money. For ten days we survived by eating canned baked beans mixed with brown sugar heated up in an electric coffee pot. Our landlady, a gruff old woman, smelled the beans, and yelled up the stairs, "Stop cooking in your room," which was one of her many house rules for students. Money was short, and I realized I could not continue my senior year at the university. But, I wouldn't let this setback deter me.

Now, more than ever, I was determined to become a naval aviator. After reapplying and being accepted for the Naval Aviation Flight Program – subject to passing a flight physical examination – I found out Milton College, ironically, was now approved for the program. After enlisting as a Seaman 2nd Class in the naval reserve and passing the flight physical, I received orders to report for preliminary flight training at the Reserve Naval Air Station Glenview, Illinois in October of 1940. Small air stations, like Glenview, located near the larger cities had a primary mission to support naval air reserve squadrons. Their secondary mission was to process and provide ten hours of flight training for prospective flight students during a thirty-day flight training period. Flight students were eliminated who couldn't adapt themselves to flying prior to being sent to a major flight school. Most of the larger cities in the United States had naval air stations similar to Glenview located in close proximity to the cities and were called Elimination Bases or "E Bases."

At Glenview, we flew yellow biplane flight trainers designated as *N3Ns,* which had been built at the Philadelphia Naval Aircraft Factory. It was a rugged, safe aircraft, but I had one scary incident. My flight instructor was demonstrating the emergency procedure to be used if the plane's engine suddenly quit. The first action would be to immediately push the control stick forward to get the nose of the plane down from level flight. With the nose down, sufficient air speed was maintained to prevent the plane from stalling out or going out of control. The first two times my instructor simulated an engine failure by suddenly cutting off the engine throttle, I was slow getting the plane's nose down. The next day when my instructor abruptly cut the throttle, I was determined to get the nose down fast. Quickly, I jammed the control stick forward and immediately found myself tightly gripping it with both hands just to stay in the cockpit. My safety belt was unhooked! The plane was about 800 feet above the ground and was too low to use my parachute. The instructor was satisfied with my maneuver, but never knew how close he came to losing his student.

N3N primary flight trainer - Flight student Fisher

Most flight students needed the full ten hours of flight training to qualify for solo flight. The weather at Glenview had deteriorated the last week of our thirty-day training period and all training flights had been cancelled. Consequently, I was concerned I'd be eliminated from the flight program because I hadn't yet soloed. After a suspenseful week of worrying about my fate, my instructor told me I'd flown well enough without soloing and recommended I continue flight training at Pensacola. Instead of Pensacola, I received my orders for flight training at the new naval air station in Jacksonville, Florida, starting 10 January 1941. After reporting I would be designated a Naval Aviation Cadet and paid seventy-five dollars a month.

I knew now that I was truly leaving home. On a frigid night in January, my dad, grandpa and I piled into the family's 1937 "Chevy" and headed to the train station for my departure to Jacksonville. I thought my dad was brave to hand me the car keys because the city streets were coated with sheer ice. I didn't think I was driving that fast, but suddenly without warning, the old Chevy spun around in a 270-degree circle, went backwards over the curb, passed between two stately oaks, and finally came to an abrupt halt in a snow bank. Not a word was said as I guided the Chevy back onto the street and continued our trip with a little bit more caution. The rest of the drive was uneventful. After a three-hour wait for the delayed train, it was time to say goodbye. I hugged Dad and Grandpa and boarded the train to Jacksonville with great anticipation.

The train ride was uneventful and dull. Because I was the only passenger in my coach, there was no one else to talk to except the black Pullman porter. After arriving at the railroad station at Jacksonville and entering the station, I found out the South was very different from the North. There were signs posted for separate "white" and "black" drinking fountains and toilets. After boarding a practically empty bus heading to the naval air station, I sat down in a row of seats just ahead of some middle-aged black women. The bus driver scowled at me and motioned for me to move forward saying, "Hey Buddy, you can't sit there." So dragging my suitcase, I moved to the front of the bus. I had been sitting in the black segregated area. This *Dammed Yankee* was rapidly getting educated.

CHAPTER 2
FLIGHT TRAINING

Primary Flight Training

After arriving at the Jacksonville Naval Air Station in Florida the second week of January 1941, I submitted my orders to the duty officer at the Aviation Cadet Regimental headquarters and was assigned to flight class 1-B-41-J. My flight class would be the second flight class to commence primary flight training at the new air station. After walking over to the cadet barracks, I located my assigned room and met my new roommate. He shook my hand, and said, "I'm Andrew Jackson Loundes the Third," and I answered, "I'm Clayton Fisher." Then I innocently said, "You sure have a funny name." He looked at me and said, "Fisher, my name isn't any funnier than your suit."

I was wearing a dark olive-green covert cloth suit purchased from a local haberdasher before leaving for Florida. I had my mind set on a dark tan, covert cloth suit, but they had sold out. The wily haberdasher didn't want to lose a sale, so he talked me into buying the green suit. Andy and I again shook hands, and we both started laughing. That humorous exchange was the beginning of a close friendship. Andy was from Baltimore. He had graduated from the University of Virginia and had been a fraternity boy. He had worked for the Reynolds Tobacco Company and told me he'd never been west of Kentucky. When I told him, I was from Wisconsin, he laughed and told me, "You must have lived in Indian country." I thought, "What a contrast – Andy, the sophisticated fraternity boy, and me, the small-town country boy."

Aviation Cadet Fisher - Flight Class 1B41J - U.S. Navy photo

Andy's parents were members of the posh Ponte Vedra Country Club near Jacksonville Beach and this was where he intended to spend his weekends with his girlfriend from Baltimore. However, Andy had a problem with a couple of our aviation-cadet regiment naval officers who also spent their weekends at the country club. Those two officers started a hazing program against Andy by giving him demerits for various infractions for the condition of our room. The officers inspected the cadets' rooms daily, except weekends. Andy and I rotated cleaning our room each day, and signed a sheet to indicate which cadet had done the cleaning. Andy always received demerits the day he signed the inspection sheet, regardless of how well he cleaned our room. I never received any demerits when I signed the sheet even if the room was slightly messy. It took two hours to walk off a demerit; actually, it took two hours walking carrying a rifle and was on Saturday mornings. This was highly inconvenient to Andy because it cut into his weekend time at the country club. The majority of the time I would stay aboard the air station on Saturdays, so, as a favor to Andy, I would sign his name to the posted list of cadets with demerits, check out a rifle and walk off his demerits. Those regimental officers never caught on!

The air station was so new that the flight-training program was in its infancy and still being organized. Shortly, after I arrived, I checked out the aircraft hangers to look at the new yellow Stearman *N2S* primary trainers I would be flying. Then I noticed coffins stacked up in one corner. Seeing all those coffins was a shock, but why so many? The answer would be obvious in months to come.

Finally in February, it was time to climb into those yellow birds and start flight training. Because of a shortage of experienced flight instructors, some naval aviators who had recently graduated from the flight program were assigned as primary flight instructors. They called these instructors "plough backs" and unfortunately I drew a plough back.

The voice communication between the instructor and flight student was a one-way communication. The student wore a special flight helmet connected to a hollow voice tube called the "Gosport," a tube invented in Gosport, England. Only the instructor could talk to his student which allowed this system of no questions or excuses from the student.

On my first training flight, returning back to the air station, my novice flight instructor turned our plane sharply and into a very steep glide and aimed the plane at a small farmyard filled with white Leghorn chickens. As our plane approached at about a thirty-foot altitude, chickens and feathers were flying in all directions. I could empathize with those panicked chickens remembering my childhood experience with my "huge bird." This kind of low flying was illegal and called "flat-hatting." He pulled this stunt a few more times on other flights, and I wouldn't have blamed the farmer if he had peppered our plane with shotgun pellets.

Part of our primary training was practicing precision turns flying around two ground pylons. These pylons were spaced so you had to make tight turns in an unbroken figure-eight pattern while flying at 500 feet. This precision maneuver taught us how to make smooth right and left turns. These maneuvers were dangerous if you pulled back your control stick too hard during a tight turn while maintaining an unbroken figure-eight pattern. You could stall out your lower wing and spin your aircraft into the ground. At this stage of training, we had our first student fatality. It was a shock and a wake-up call to all of us. Flying was not all fun and games and could be deadly if you made a mistake during this maneuver.

You had to fly three pre-solo flight checks by different flight instructors before you could solo. Then you had to fly two "up checks" out of the three checks. Up-checks are indicated when the flight instructor lifts his thumb in the traditional gesture of success. In addition, you had to demonstrate you could safely handle crosswind landings. My novice flight instructor had me turn the plane into the crosswind with the wings level to the runway and then line the plane up parallel to the runway before the wheels hit. The timing had to be almost perfect in a crosswind to keep the plane from drifting laterally. If the aircraft was drifting when the wheels hit, you could "ground loop" and tear up a wing. Fortunately, I drew an experienced flight instructor for my first flight check who'd recently returned from a fleet aircraft squadron. After my first attempt at a crosswind landing, he promptly gave me a down check and told me he was going to use the time to teach me how to correctly handle crosswind landings. He had me crab into the crosswind by dropping a wing and then skidding the plane into the crosswind. He told me, "Just do everything you can, so you're not drifting sideways." The instructors name was LTJG "Smoke" Strean. He became a highly respected combat pilot and, later in his career, became a vice admiral.

In March, I was cleared for my solo flight after receiving up checks on my last two solo checks. During the solo flight, a fairly strong crosswind developed, and the control tower hoisted a single round ball, a visual signal, for all students to land. Then a two-ball signal was hoisted notifying instructors with students to land. There were no radios in the primary trainer for the control tower to communicate with the pilots. The areas between the new runways were sandy and I could see sand blowing and streaming across the runway at about a 30 degree angle. I was scared, but managed to make a successful crosswind landing. LTJG Strean's crosswind-landing instructions were going to save my butt a few more times later in my flight career. To this day as a passenger, I'm always aware of how the pilots of modern jet airliners handle crosswind landings.

Early one morning, the regiment commander cancelled all flight training, ordered us to dress in our khaki uniforms, join our regiment and then march in formation to the parade ground. To our surprise, President Franklin D. Roosevelt was sitting in an open convertible limousine on the road bordering the field. He proceeded to praise our ambition and service as future naval aviators. He announced the Navy's plan to train 10,000 naval aviators! It was an ominous statement, meaning we may soon be involved in the war in Europe.

The final and last flight check for the primary flight stage was "Shooting the Circle." This tested a student's ability to safely land the plane in a prescribed area in the event of engine failure. A circle with about a 200-foot diameter was marked on one of our auxiliary flight training fields. Your instructor flew you around the outer perimeter of the field at an 800-foot altitude and would suddenly cut off the engine throttle at various positions on the perimeter of the field. Then he demonstrated how to land the plane within the circle. First, he would do shallow "S" turns while descending, either widening or narrowing the turns as he determined whether he was too high or too low, as he was closing the distance to the circle. In the final approach it was always better to be too high, than too low. When he was too high, he would side slip the plane by dipping either the right or left wing down and then kicking in the opposite directional rudder. This maneuver would sharply increase the rate of descent to kill off excess altitude. If he was too low and the plane had enough excess air speed, he would gently pull the nose of the plane up to slow its descent and hope the plane reached the circle before it settled into the ground. Correctly determining the wind velocity was a big factor in successfully shooting the circle.

After enough practice with your instructor and he thought you were ready for your check ride, he landed, got out of the plane and stood on the side of the field to watch you fly your check flight. You had to hit inside the circle at least four out of six attempts, I hit five out of five for an up check on my first attempt, and I then landed to pick up my instructor. Then we both watched other students trying to hit the circle. There were some weird maneuvers as some students desperately tried to recover high positions to hit the circle. They'd almost crash their plane to hit that circle.

Final primary check in N2S aircraft- 'Shooting the Circle'
Courtesy Bob Rasmussen

After I successfully completed my primary stage of flight training, the fear and pressure of "Washing out" was now over.

Basic Flight Training

On 6 May, I entered basic flight training. I was through flying the "Yellow Perils" and would be flying monoplanes at Lee Field, an auxiliary flight facility near the Jacksonville air station. Naval aviation was going through a major transition from biplanes to monoplanes in both the fleet squadrons and the various flight training commands. The monoplanes had different wing stall characteristics and would stall quicker than in the biplanes. The flight instructor's main concern was preventing his students from getting into dangerous situations, especially in landings. My instructor who checked me out in the North American *SNJ* basic trainer had taken control away from me a couple times in my final approaches. He was worried about my slow air speed on my final landing approach coupled with cutting the throttle off too soon as I started to flare out for the final part of the landing. An air speed too slow could stall out the aircraft and drop a wing into the runway. Looking back, I was making good solid landings almost similar to my later aircraft carrier landing.

During basic training, I almost terminated my flight career. It was a cold morning and my instructor kept yelling at me when I had trouble starting my engine. After we got airborne, I could do nothing right and the entire flight was a nightmare. On my next scheduled flight with the same instructor, he again was in a sour mood and glared at me as he climbed into the rear cockpit. After flying him a good solid flight, I felt proud of myself. When we landed, he told me, "You're getting a down check, Fisher." I asked "Why?" He scowled and said, "You didn't have your seat belt hooked." Albeit, it was an oversight on my part, he should have exercised more responsibility when he first noticed it was unhooked, instead of endangering my safety. The next day, I flew another good flight. When we returned to Lee Field and entered the flight pattern around the field, there were numerous yellow primary-flight trainers circling at 1,000 feet. Because it was easier to see the other aircraft from our monoplanes unobstructed view upward, circling above us at 1,000 feet, I decided to descend to a slightly lower altitude. My instructor went ballistic, screaming at me to stay at the prescribed altitude and trying to take control of the aircraft. We had a little tug–of–war for control of the control stick and I lost. Losing that little war got me another down check. This meant I would have too fly three more flight checks, if the squadron commander recommended me for extra time.

Deciding I had been pushed too far; I was not going to put up with being brow beaten anymore by this instructor. Angry and upset, I was not thinking very rationally when I walked into the squadron office and told the squadron commander I refused to fly anymore with my instructor and wanted out of the training program. The squadron commander quietly listened to me and said, "Why don't you step outside of the office for ten minutes then come back and tell me if you still want to quit flying." After leaving the office, I cooled down and realized how foolish I had been. When I walked back in the commander's office, I told him I still wanted to fly. I completed my basic training on 20 June after being assigned a new instructor and easily passed the various remaining check flights.

Operational Flight Training

The big crossroad in my flight career was just ahead. After finishing basic training, I had requested operational flight training for multi-engine seaplanes at Pensacola; instead, I received orders for carrier operational flight training at the naval air station Opa Locke, Florida, where I would become an aircraft carrier pilot, a "Tailhooker." It took me a couple days adjusting to the reality that I was not going to fly multi-engine seaplanes. But, this change didn't quell my growing excitement that I would instead be flying fighter planes. So with great anticipation, I drove down to Opa Locke, Florida in my old Buick sedan I had purchased in Jacksonville.

Carrier operational flight training was going to be a somewhat dangerous, but exciting experience; I would learn acrobatics, aerial gunnery, dive bombing, night flying and night cross-country navigation flights right over the middle of the Florida Everglades, with their alligators and cottonmouth snakes. If we had to bail out over the Everglades, we were jokingly told, spread out your parachute, sit in it, get a stick and beat off the snakes. In 1941, the Everglades were very wet and looked ominous from the air, with its mostly green slimy muck.

On 25 June, I flew my first operational training flight in an obsolete aircraft, a little Boeing *F4B-4* biplane fighter with a big radial engine.

It was small, but very maneuverable. When I stuck my arm out of the cockpit, I could make the fighter do a slight turn. Next, I checked out in a stubby, Grumman *F3F-3* fighter biplane, which on takeoffs made a high-pitched noise, reminding me of a huge bumblebee. This aircraft had a retractable landing gear and it took over twenty turns to hand crank the wheels up. Your cockpit checkoff list for landing became a little more important because you didn't want to be embarrassed with wheels-up landing.

Grumann F3F-3 Fighter - U.S. Navy photo

We practiced dog fighting by pairing off with another student. At 8,000 feet, we would approach each other's aircraft going in opposite directions. As we passed, we both tried to make the smoothest 180-degree tight turn to gain the advantage by getting in a tail position on your adversary and then, theoretically, shoot him down. As combatants, we flew exactly the same type fighter, so neither pilot had an advantage of flying a superior fighter. We had to rely on own flight skills. It was very difficult to get in a shoot-down position. Most student dogfights usually ended in a draw, but an exceptionally skilled flight student would win most of his dogfights. Life is not always fair.

Practicing aerial gunnery over the Everglades doing deflection shooting was probably the high point of my operational training. We fired 30-caliber machine guns at a white cylindrical target sleeve towed by another fighter. We did three types of defection shooting: overhead, high-side and flat-side runs. On the overhead run, you flew some distance ahead of the tow plane, did a fairly tight reverse turn while rolling over on your back, and pulled the nose of your plane down to pick up the tow line and white target sleeve. The high-side run started by setting some distance ahead and above the tow aircraft, either to the right or left side. Then you started a 180-degree turn to reverse course, while descending at about 50 degrees and then turning toward the towline to pick up the target. Doing the flat-side run, you again made a 180-degree turn, but at the same altitude as the tow plane and turned toward the towline until you could to see the target. These gunnery runs set you up with various degrees of deflection shots at the target. Aerial gunnery, especially deflection shooting took a lot of practice. We were just learning the basics.

The Grumman *F3F-3* fighter had a very bad flight characteristic of going into a vicious inverted outside tailspin if you pulled too tight a turn, especially doing the over-head gunnery run. In the inverted spin, the aircraft is partially on its back and spinning in a tight circle with the pilot facing toward the outside of the circle. The centrifugal force would throw you out of the cockpit without your seat belt. An inside-spin which is less violent, the pilot is facing the inside of the circle of the spin and is pushed hard against the seat. To recover from the outside-spin, you had to get the nose pointing down by pulling back hard on the control stick to stop the spin. There had been several unfortunate flight-student mishaps resulting in loss of life and aircraft. It had been determined that during the outside-inverted spin recovery, the pilot thought he was pulling the control stick back, but was actually pulling out on the joystick due to the very strong centrifugal forces. In addition, aircraft were being lost because the students were panicking and bailing out too soon.

Before one gunnery flight, our instructor briefed us about the importance of making several attempts to recover from inverted spins, emphasizing, "Don't bail out too soon." During the flight, the instructor's aircraft went into the dreaded inverted - outside spin while he was doing an over-head run. He bailed out at about 3,000 feet and we watched him slowly descend into the Everglades close to a road, now called "Alligator Alley." We saw a black line trailing behind him as he struggled to walk in waist-high green muck to the road. During this spectacle, lively chatter crackled over our radios about how quick our instructor had bailed out, one student yelled, "Look at the poor bastard plowing through that muck!" The next day our instructor, sporting a black eye, never spoke again about bailing out too soon or about his experience in the swamp.

We first learned to do steep dive-bombing runs in the *F3F-3* fighter aiming at a circular target on the ground. We dropped miniature smoke-bombs from a rack under a wing so we could see our bombing results. The fighter didn't have dive brakes to slow down the aircraft in a dive, but the biplanes wings provided sufficient air resistance to maintain a slow enough speed for dive bombing. As you gained experience in dive bombing you were able to judge your rapidly changing altitude by seeing ground objects change in size and become more distinguishable. In the dive, you alternated between looking through your telescope sight and taking quick glimpses of your rapidly unwinding altimeter indicators. On one dive-bombing run, I had "Target fixation," I was gazing at the target too long and suddenly realized I was getting too low. As I pulled back hard on the control stick to recover from the dive, the nose of the aircraft came up, and I had the sensation of being in a big saucer looking up at its edge. Now, that was being too low. After fully recovering from the dive and regaining level flight, the impact of what I had done hit home. That day I had almost become a student fatality.

In a letter to my sister, I described my progress in flight training and my enthusiasm for acrobatics:

> *"Stunt flying is a bit of physical labor, jerking the control stick around and kicking the rudder pedals. At first I would lose my*

sense of direction and get a little dizzy, but I'm getting air-minded and know my way around most stunts. I can do loops, slow rolls barrel rolls, wingovers, split S's, and Immelman turns. Another student and I went up and watched each other's stunts while flying parallel. It's fun to watch the other plane's maneuver develop when you're close to the plane.

Aviation will make me unfit for the humdrum and conventional life. It's an exciting life flying, and it's a chance to see some of the world. I hope the price isn't too great in the end, but I want to stick with it."

Flying was not all fun and games, and to ease the tension, a little social life was in order. During the summer season in the Miami area, the Hollywood Beach Hotel, a famous hotel in the city of Hollywood, offered the aviation cadets special reduced summer rates for hotel services and bar drinks if we wore our white uniforms with those single gold stars on our black shoulder bars. It seemed they wanted a little color around the Hotel. We jokingly called ourselves "One Star Admirals." Wearing those white uniforms for social events at the hotel wasn't too bad a deal because we could get our uniforms laundered at the air base laundry for ten cents each. The Hotel also let cadets run a bar tab that you didn't have to pay until you finished flight training and you were commissioned an officer. After being commissioned, we were entitled to a $1,000 allowance to buy our officer uniforms and other required paraphernalia. Anyway, when I graduated on 8 August 1941, I had an officer's commission, those coveted gold wings, my uniform allowance and an unpaid bar bill at the Hollywood Beach Hotel. To get out of town I had to use a good chunk of my uniform allowance to settle with the Hotel.

The cadets had weekends off at Opa Locka, but we had a 2100 curfew during the week through Thursday and then Sunday night. The cadet's social life was confined to Friday and Saturday nights because of the curfew. One Saturday afternoon, I was lying on my bunk with the door open. One of my fellow flight students stuck his head in my room and asked me if I wanted a blind date. Normally, I spent most of my Friday and Saturday evenings out with other cadets, and I wasn't sure I wanted to become involved with an unknown date. Anyway, I agreed to the blind date, put on my white uniform, and met my friends who were waiting for me outside our barracks in the cadet's car. My date was a well-built blonde with an outgoing personality. We piled into the car and headed for the Hollywood Beach Hotel. At the hotel, they had an open-air terrace with a dance band and beach cabanas where we sipped rum and coke drinks called Cuba Libras. At the time, there was a popular song called *Moon over Miami,* and sometimes we were treated to spectacular full moons. Anyway, it was usually too warm to dance very much, so most of the cadet crowd sat around in the cabanas drinking those rum and cokes. The sandy beach in front of the cabanas was the home of sand crabs called sand fiddlers. As the sun went down these creatures popped up out of the sand and ran all over the beach area. They had beady eyes and ran somewhat sideways with their long legs in a funny gait. Sometimes, we had to chase them away from our cabanas. After that enjoyable fun evening, I continued dating the blonde and consequently my hotel total bar tab increased astronomically.

The day after my flight class had completed flight training, the senior flight-training officer told the class to line up at noon in front of the base administration building, and the base commander would hand each student his officer's commission as an ensign in the naval reserve and then pin on his gold wings.

For some reason, maybe due to my recent social life, I had not passed the radio-code requirements. When I told the senior training officer I had not passed the final radio-code examination he picked up the telephone, called the squadron's chief radioman and told him, "I'm sending Cadet Fisher up right now for a radio-code examination and he better pass it!" The chief radioman watched me copy a few minutes of Morse code he was sending me and after checking my results, he said, "Change all your code letter H's you have written to S's. After I made the changes, he quickly graded my examination. Presto, I had passed! The letter H in code was four "dits," S was three "dits." My problem with previous exams had always been distinguishing between H's and S's. Two hours later, I had my officer's commission and those coveted gold wings.

Ten cadets from our flight class received orders to various carrier squadrons. Most of us had hoped for assignment to a fighter squadron, but my orders were to report to Bombing Squadron Eight assigned to the new aircraft carrier, the *USS Hornet,* based at Norfolk, Virginia. Ensign Grant Teats from our flight class had orders to Torpedo Squadron Eight. Grant would be shot down and killed in the Battle of Midway 4 June 1942. Only one pilot in his squadron survived the battle. I think they assigned pilots from our little flight class to the Hornet air group by name in alphabetical order. The name Fisher was higher on the alphabet than Teats.

With thirty days leave before reporting to my squadron, I drove home to Janesville, Wisconsin. When I walked into the house, Peter, my mixed-breed collie, circled me for a long time, barking furiously at this strange intruder, until he recognized me.

The reunion with my dog "Peter"

After being home a couple weeks, I began missing flying and the camaraderie that existed among the aviators. My parents worried about me flying, but they never tried to influence any of my career decisions. This would be the last time I would see my father after I departed for Norfolk. My father would die unexpectedly of a heart attack on 10 February 1942.

CHAPTER 3
BOMBING SQUADRON EIGHT

After arriving and reporting into my squadron at Norfolk Naval Air Station, the first week of September, I was anxious to go aboard the *Hornet*.

Having never been aboard a Navy ship, it was exciting standing on the dock staring up at the ship's huge island structure. After walking up the gangplank and stepping on the quarter deck, I paused wondering what to do next. Then noticing an officer standing by a podium I approached him and said, "Hello, I'm Ensign Fisher assigned to Bombing Squadron Eight." This behavior violated an age-old protocol procedure: All naval officers and enlisted personnel are to pause momentarily as they step on the quarterdeck, stand at attention facing the ship's stern and then salute the American flag flying from the stern mast. You then approach the quarter deck officer, stop, salute him and say "Request permission to come aboard." The officer returns your salute and responds, "Permission granted." In my case, the officer was probably aware that I was a young "green" aviation officer and just said, "Welcome aboard."

The *Hornet's* Air Group Commander, CDR Ring, happened to be standing next to the quarter deck officer and introduced himself to me. After I managed to salute him, the Commander shook my hand. He was a very impressive looking officer in his aviation green uniform and the gold braid on his cap. He gave me a tour of the enormous hanger and flight decks. As we were walking on the hanger deck, we passed a *Curtiss SBC-4* dive bomber tied down to the deck. The plane had the letters CHAG, the abbreviation for Commander Hornet Air Group, painted on the side of the plane in large black letters. This was the Commander's plane. It was obvious the aircraft had made a hard landing. Its landing gear was collapsed, and the wings were drooping because the main wing's bracing wires were broken. The Commander never mentioned who the pilot was that had wrecked the plane, but I speculated the Commander had probably wanted to make the very first landing on the *Hornet*.

The *Hornet's* Air Group's four squadrons would be organized and trained at the Norfolk naval air station. For additional dive-bombing practice, new squadron pilots were temporarily ordered to a flight-training unit, stationed at Chambers Field, a small air facility bordering on Willoughby Bay. Later, the squadrons would operate from the air station's East Field. The field had two large hangers and long runways. The *Hornet's* squadrons would occupy one of the hangers.

On 3 September, I flew my first familiarization flight in a squadron *Curtiss SBC-4 "Helldiver"* dive bomber. After the familiarization flights, we practiced formation flying and dive bombing. We practiced dive bombing by dropping miniature smoke bombs on circular targets with a solid-center circle for the bull's eye. These dives started at 10,000 feet by rolling the plane into an almost vertical dive. The plane was in a vertical position but its flight path, called the track, was 70 degrees. At 70 degrees, your butt was not pushing against the seat and you were not hanging against the seat safety belt. You felt like you were floating between the belt and seat. We had competition among the squadron pilots trying to get the most bull's-eyes. The secret to getting bull's-eyes was the pilot's ability to prevent the plane from skidding laterally in the dive. Because of the plane's constantly changing air speed, you had to continuously adjust the plane's rudder-trim tab in the dive. In addition, the direction and velocity of the wind required adjustment of your lead as you sighted the target through the plane's telescope.

All squadron pilots who had never made a carrier landing attended ground training sessions to learn the fundamentals of carrier landings. Carrier landings require a pilot to fly the airplane in level flight with its wheels and landing flaps down at about 10 knots above its stalling speed, a departure from the normal 15 knots drilled into every flight student. The Landing Signal Officer ("LSO"), an experienced carrier pilot, demonstrated the various signals that assisted the pilot in making the carrier landings, by using his arms while holding square-shaped framed flags — nicknamed "paddles" — that were covered with yellow and red-colored strips of cloth. Some of the LSO's flag signals were derived from semaphore flag signals, which were used by Navy communication signalmen for transmitting visual light messages between ships.

For the flag signal "roger," derived from the phonetic radio code "R," the signalman holds both flags horizontally from his body. If the LSO gives you a steady roger, your plane is at the correct speed and altitude. Pilots prided themselves on receiving a steady roger during the final landing approach. When the LSO gives the "cut" signal by swinging his right arm and flag across his neck, this indicates to the pilot to pull his throttle off. If you're too high, the LSO holds his arms and flags up in a "V" position and gradually lowers his arms to a roger position as you correct your altitude. If you're too low, the LSO lowers his arms in an inverted V signal and raises his arms up to the roger position as you correct your altitude.

The most dangerous situation for a pilot is being too slow or too low. For the "slow" signal, the LSO extends his arms parallel and horizontal in front of his torso then rapidly pulls his arms back to their original horizontally position. If the plane is too fast, the LSO hits his right paddle against the side of his leg. The LSO also slants his arms and paddles in a diagonal position right or left to indicate you are not lined with up with the center of the flight deck, or the white line marked on the practice fields. The only mandatory signal is the "wave off" shown by the LSO repeatedly crossing his arms and paddles from a "V" position above his head. There are two cardinal sins for carrier pilots: taking your own cut or trying to take off after your tailhook had missed hooking on to the arresting gear cables. The cables used to snag the plane's tailhook are more commonly called "wires" by pilots and flight deck personnel. If your tailhook fails to engage a wire, your plane could crash into a barrier which consists of three cables attached to vertical stanchions, positioned a few feet ahead of the last arresting gear wire. The crash barrier's normal position is flat on the flight deck. It is then elevated up just before each carrier landing. If a plane fails to catch a wire and if the pilot tries to take off again, his plane could clear the crash barrier and crash into another aircraft still taxiing forward, or into other parked aircraft. These types of crashes could badly injure or kill pilots and flight-deck personnel. Another horrible accident on a flight deck occurs when an arresting wire breaks when an airplane lands. If the wire snaps, it whips across the flight deck with such force that it can cut the legs off at the knees of a flight-deck person standing in its way.

Although, the crash barrier saved the lives of many pilots and flight deck personnel, a rare and terrible accident happened to the executive officer of a fighter squadron. After landing on the *U.S.S. Enterprise* during the war in 1942, he was decapitated by the propeller blade of another fighter when it bounced high over the crash barrier and landed on top of his plane.

On 24 September, another squadron pilot and I flew a dive bomber from the air station to practice our first carrier landings called FCLP's on a practice grass field located in the farm lands about twenty miles west of Norfolk. This entailed crossing the *Great Dismal Swamp* known to be infested with poisonous snakes, not a happy thought.

After landing at the practice field, one pilot would get out of the plane and observe the other pilot's landings. During these practice landings, you can't carry a passenger until you've become a carrier-qualified pilot by completing eight successful carrier landings. Believe me, your first few attempts at getting your plane's airspeed down to 80 knots while flying low over trees is hairy and scary. Most of the LSO's signals the novice pilots received were the "too fast" and "too high" signals. During FCLP, as you gradually gained more confidence and experience, you finally started "riding the roger" until you received the cut signal to land.

When we completed that first day of FCLP, I piloted the plane and headed back to Norfolk. As we were flying over some of the worst looking parts of the swamp, I was thinking, "Engine don't quit now." Suddenly, my engine lost power. When I grabbed the handle of the gas valve to shift to another gas tank, I heard my passenger giggling over the intercom radio. The plane had dual controls, and my "jokester" passenger had slyly eased off the engine throttle. With my hand off the throttle, I didn't feel the throttle pull off. Believing that there was truly a problem, I thought we might end up in the swamp fending off snakes. It took me a few minutes before I found any humor in his prank.

A few weeks later on a Sunday afternoon in October, I was sitting in the lounge of the air station's Officers Club when who walks in but the *jokester* pilot from *The Dismal Swamp* episode. He was with another squadron pilot and the pilot's wife, but what really received my attention, was a striking and attractive looking girl he was escorting. After being introduced to the girl, her name was Anne Koster, and she was a Second Lieutenant in the Army Nursing Corps, stationed at Fort Story, Virginia Beach, and had been employed at Doctors Hospital in Washington D.C. before entering the Army. Eleanor Roosevelt had invited nurses from the Washington area hospitals for teas in the White House to recruit them for the Army and Navy. At the time, I erroneously assumed she was his date, so I decided to needle him by trying to get a date with her. Turning the back of my chair around and facing her with my arms on the chair's back, I launched my pitch. The more I talked, the more she parried me. After much joking and teasing, she finally gave me her telephone number. Little did I know at that moment that I would later lose my bachelorhood by marrying Annie.

Two British aircraft carriers, the *HMS Formidable* and the *HMS Illustrious,* were in the Newport News shipyards being repaired due to major battle damage caused by air attacks from German Junkers *Ju87Stuka* dive bombers near the islands of Malta and Crete. While in port, the officers and enlisted men from these carriers were going to play rugby and soccer football games on the evening of 15 October, at Foreman Field in Norfolk. I bought two tickets for this event at the great cost of fifty cents per ticket.

HOOKED

Anne Koster at Doctors Hospital in Washington, D.C., 1940

On the following Monday, I called Annie and told her about the games. Lucky for me she was interested in most sports, and I had a date. The soccer game played by the enlisted men was dull and not too interesting, but the fierce competition between the officer rugby players impressed us, especially since they didn't wear protective padding. After our date, Annie told me that an Army officer had asked her for a date shortly after she had accepted my date. She told him she already had a date with a Navy pilot at 1900 and if he didn't show up by 1905 she would go out with him. Since it was my first date, I thought it would be prudent to be on time, so I arrived at her quarters at 1855. If she had stood me up that evening, I wouldn't have asked her for another date. Our two daughters were fascinated when they heard the story of how close they came to not existing. To get ahead of my story, we did continue to date and I asked her to marry me on 28 November using a pay phone at the Columbia Municipal airport in South Carolina. She did not accept my proposal until after I had arrived back at Norfolk.

Our squadron had participated in Army maneuvers near Fort Bragg, South Carolina in November of 1941 and two large armies called the Red and Blue had conducted the maneuvers. The German Stuka dive bombers had been very effective in Europe and our Air Corps at that time did not have dive-bomber squadrons. So, Bombing Squadron 8 was assigned to the Red Army to participate in the maneuvers and to add more realism. On 10 November, the squadron departed from Norfolk and landed at the Columbia Municipal Airport where the squadron would operate along with an Army Air Corps squadron flying new *P-38* twin-engine fighters. What a contrast in aircraft, our obsolete biplane *Curtiss SBC-4* dive bombers and those sleek modern fighters. Times like this I wondered why I had chosen to be a naval aviator.

The two squadrons had a conflict in their standard flight landing patterns around the airfield. Navy pilots used a standard carrier landing pattern, making a tight turn at about five hundred feet on our final approach to the runway at 85 knots. The *P-38* pilots made very long straight- in approaches to land at over 100 knots. And because of this, the landing times for both squadrons returning from flight missions couldn't be coordinated. After a couple of near misses during landings between our dive bombers and the *P-38s,* our squadron commander and the *P-38's* squadron commander met to discuss the problem. They decided the Navy pilots would give way to the landing *P-38s* in all landing situations because the P-38 pilots were greener than the Navy pilots! At Fort Bragg, our squadron personnel were quartered in Army barracks. The barracks were heated by pot-bellied coal burning heaters, but only in the morning. Those nights in South Carolina were damp and very cold and the pilots ended up sleeping under blankets over winter flight suits, and then to wake up and find a thick coating of ice on the vehicle's windshields. Surprisingly by noon, it was warm enough for the pilots and our air-crewmen to play softball on the airfield.

On our flight missions, we simulated low-level bombing and strafing attacks on the Blue Army's trucks, troops caught on the roads and dive bombing bridges. While returning from a bombing mission on Thanksgiving Day, I noticed cars clustered around farmhouses where families and relatives were enjoying their turkey dinners. So for kicks, I decided to do a dive-bombing run on a farmhouse surrounded by many parked cars. I put my propeller in the low-pitch position for the dive because it made a very high-pitched sound. After diving, I pulled out very low, thinking it was great sport at the time. Thinking back, I now realize my shenanigans might have caused a heart attack of an elderly person. At the Columbia airport our planes were parked on grass and dirt surfaces, and when we taxied to the takeoff runway, the planes' propellers raised clouds of dust that sucked into our engines. This gritty dust had started to damage our engine's piston rings which caused the engines to burn some engine oil. This became apparent, while flying formation, when you flew through streams of black smoke from the planes ahead of you. The squadron managed to fly all our planes back to Norfolk on 28 November without incident and all the engines had to be changed.

Curtiss SBC-4 dive bomber - U.S. Navy photo

The new Breeze Point bachelor officer's quarters were filled up, so some officers were allowed to live off the air station. Ensign "KB" White, my roommate on the *Hornet*, and I rented a room in a residential home in Norfolk. I was the squadron duty officer on Sunday 7 December, a telephone watch, in case of any squadron problems. That Sunday morning, resting on my bed, listening to soft music on the radio and reading a newspaper, my tranquil morning was shattered when the music was abruptly interrupted and the radio announcer excitingly saying, "Pearl Harbor has just been attacked by Japanese carrier based dive bombers and torpedo bombers!" My first thought was where the hell is Pearl Harbor? Totally stunned, then angered by the sneak attack, we were now at war. Our air group and the *Hornet* would soon be joining the Pacific Fleet.

A squadron pilot called and told me all pilots were to report immediately to the squadron. A Colt 45-caliber pistol with its belt and holster was issued to each pilot. Frankly, I didn't know why we needed these guns; maybe they were symbolic of our warrior status. At meal times, our gun belts with guns and uniform caps hung on hooks just outside the dining area; a look reminiscent of the old wild west. The guns would become our constant companions when we flew off the *Hornet*. My gun was going to survive two major carrier battles and a ditching of my dive bomber in the south Pacific

In late October, Annie learned her mother had terminal cancer. She used up the few leave days she had accumulated in her short military career to be at her mother's side at her home in Iowa. Annie had requested a discharge from the Army, so she could return home to nurse her mother. On 8 December, she received a telegram that her request for discharge was going to be disallowed. The next day, she received another wire stating since her discharge had already been approved on 6 December, it was her choice, stay in or get out, it was patriotism versus love and loyalty to her mother. She accepted a discharge that was effective 6 January 1942.

This decision may have saved her life. Annie's medical team cadre was deployed to a field hospital located on a beachhead at Salerno, Italy, where General Clark's troops had successfully landed. The

Germans counter-attacked and almost re-captured the beachhead, but in the process, the beach casualty hospital suffered many medical personnel casualties when German *Stuka* dive bombers hit the hospital area. The cadre's head surgeon had a leg blown off.

CHAPTER 4
HORNET'S SHAKE DOWN CRUISE

Gulf of Mexico

The *Hornet* was formally commissioned 21 October at NAS Norfolk. She was now the newest aircraft carrier in the fleet and with the latest innovations. On a short trial run at sea, I was a passenger in the rear seat of a squadron plane being flown out to land on the ship. The pilot was a senior squadron officer who had very little carrier landing experience, so I was very apprehensive. As we lost sight of land, we only had the horizon in our sights, which was a new experience for me. Again, I asked myself why I'd become a naval aviator, when I could have been an Army Corps aviator. The pilot made a sloppy, but safe landing, and I felt for the first time the sensation of the plane engaging its tailhook and the rapid deceleration at the end.

USS Hornet CV-9 arriving at NAS Norfolk to be commissioned 21 October 1941 - U.S. Navy photo

HOOKED

At the end of December, the *Hornet* and our air group was scheduled for a shake-down cruise in the Gulf of Mexico. Why the Gulf of Mexico? At that time, German submarines were operating off our Atlantic coast and sinking ships. Our air group's aircraft and personnel moved aboard to prepare for our first training cruise. All the ships and air group personnel were ordered to be aboard by 2000 Christmas Eve.

The *Hornet* was anchored in Hampton Roads and liberty boats were busy ferrying personnel between the air station dock and the *Hornet.* Annie drove me down to the bustling dock, where she gave me her prized record collection along with her combination radio and 78-rpm record player. At the time, I didn't realize what a wonderful gift it was and also what a great morale builder it would be for me and our squadron pilots.

The *Hornet* had a long, steep ladder rigged from the edge of the quarterdeck down to a platform that was also rigged to the side the ship. The liberty boats came along side the platform and unloaded personnel. While climbing up, it would be prudent to hang on to one of the ladder's handrails. It was going to be tough carrying the heavy box of records in both arms, while sliding my right arm against the handrail. I asked a sailor to carry the lighter-weight radio and record player. When I looked up the ladder, the distance seemed daunting. After managing to make it to the quarterdeck, my leg muscles were burning, and I was completely winded. The next morning the *Hornet* lifted anchor and the ship was underway.

The *Hornet* made a safe passage down the Atlantic coast without sighting any submarines and entered the Gulf of Mexico. Our air group's organization and training could compare to the training of an expansion baseball team. We started with a small nucleus of experienced pilots, filling out the squadron rosters with pilots who had recently received their wings. Most of the pilots had to be carrier-qualified by making eight carrier landings. The dive-bomber planes were old and obsolete and the torpedo squadron didn't have torpedo airplanes and would have to train in old training type airplanes. Later a special mission would be assigned to the *Hornet,* causing the air group to lose training time that could be compared a baseball teams spring training.

The Pearl Harbor attack accelerated our training. Each squadron had about twenty-two pilots per squadron, a fighter squadron, two dive-bomber squadrons and the torpedo squadron. All pilots had to make eight carrier landings to be carrier qualified or, for the experienced carrier pilots, to be re-qualified. About ninety pilots made over 700 landings. There were a lot of wave-offs the first few days of carrier landings. The LSO was a very busy man, beating and probably bruising his right leg, giving the fast signal. The first week's lack of progress was very discouraging to both the flight deck crews and the air group pilots. There was a number of damaged aircraft and flight deck planking that was splintered by propellers when a plane nosed over in a bad landing. One pilot was waved-off about twenty times trying to make his first landing, until he finally got the cut signal. He was almost sent back to land at the Pensacola air station.

Qualifying as a Tailhooker

I made my first carrier landing on 31 December and eight more landings the same day. On my birthday, 14 January, I made my first, night carrier landing, adding up to a grand total of twenty-three carrier landings. For a night carrier landing, you needed a clear night with enough starlight to allow you to see the carrier's silhouette from your landing pattern. None of the junior pilots had enough instrument flight experience to make a night-carrier landing on a pitch-dark night. Under this condition, the pilot had to rely mostly on his flight instruments, getting a fleeting look at the ship's lighting. Even for the experienced carrier pilots, night-carrier landings were dangerous, and the LSO had to use lighted paddles.

The LSO did an outstanding job of carrier-qualifying the air group's pilots, without a fatal accident. There was a safety net rigged below the flight-deck-level LSO's platform where the LSO could jump and, in some cases, dive into the net to avoid a plane about to crash or skim right over the LSO's platform. Even with the safety net, the LSO would not always be protected if a plane crashed into the ramp and exploded. Ramp crashes usually resulted in fires and pilot fatalities.

HOOKED

On 20 January, I'd been put under ten days "hack," a punishment for officers by being confined to their rooms aboard ship, or their quarters ashore. What had I done to be punished? At the beginning of the cruise, all the pilots had been issued "signal cards" with serial numbers, which were classified "confidential," a classification just below "secret." The cards were carried by the dive-bomber pilots while flying scouting and combat missions, and their radioman would utilize the cards information to encode radio messages.

Normally, confidential documents were kept in safes. At first, all the pilots locked their cards in individual safes in their rooms, but this was impractical, so the cards ended up in the stowage compartment under our ready room seats. The compartments had three-digit combination locks, but you had to get down on your knees and face the seat to set the combination to unlock it. Since our ready rooms normally were confined to pilots and air crew members and being at sea, there was little risk to the confidential card codes being compromised. Most of the pilots set their combination locks to all zeros and just reached down and flipped the lock open.

Being the squadron assistant communications officer, I was responsible for collecting the daily information sheets provided daily to each pilot, information needed for the day's flight operations and navigation problems. Up-to-date information was constantly being displayed on teletype screens in the front section of the ready rooms, and those daily information sheets were classified confidential. After collecting the sheets from our pilots, I stuffed them in the compartment under my seat. Periodically I put the sheets in a paper bag and burned the contents in the ship's incinerator.

After developing a head cold, I was ordered to stay out of the squadron ready room. Three days later and recovering from my cold, I was allowed to return to the ready room. In my absence, my seat compartment had filled up with pilot's confidential sheets. After stuffing all the sheets in a paper bag, not realizing that I may have accidentally included my classified signal card, I burned the bag in the ship's incinerator. A few days before the *Hornet* departed the Gulf for Norfolk, the signal cards had to be returned to the ship's communication department. After a frantic search I never found my card. Being at sea, I wasn't too worried about the card being compromised. I was in for a rude awakening. I was ordered to get in my dress blue uniform and stand outside the ship's executive officers cabin. All day I had to stand there saluting various senior ships officers, wearing their khaki working uniforms, as they entered the executive officer's cabin. They all knew I was in some kind of trouble. It was embarrassing and humiliating standing there.

Finally, after all air operations were concluded for the day, a Marine sergeant arrived and told me to follow him up to the captain's cabin. When I entered the cabin, I was a little shocked to see LCDR Johnson, my squadron commander, and CAPT Mitscher, the ship's captain, seated in their dress blue uniforms. CAPT Mitscher questioned me about the lost classified information. All I could say was I thought I had inadvertently burned the signal card. He told me I had compromised the communication codes, a court martial offense. But, he said, "Because of your youth and inexperience and that we *need* all our pilots, I'm not going to court martial you. Instead, you'll be confined to your room for ten days." Although chastened, and now in hack, I'm one relieved officer.

Being under hack is like being in solitary confinement. You are allowed to eat in the officer's wardroom, but no one told me I was entitled to an hour a day for exercise. One pilot in our squadron seemed to enjoy heckling me while I was eating in the wardroom, telling me, "You're not supposed to talk to anyone while in hack." This irritated the hell out of me, and his heckling had me wondering if he had destroyed my classified signal card. The signal card was printed on heavy stock paper material, and if it had been mixed with those thin daily information sheets, I should have noticed the card. The last time I had seen the card, it was underneath my flight helmet and gloves in the seat compartment.

Being in hack commenced being punishment when my eyes became tired from reading, and hearing the same songs over-and-over on the record player was monotonous and boring. Hoping for some stimulating conversation, but denied as my roommate, exhausted from flying, would fall off to sleep while I yapped away. After about the seventh day, I wasn't able to sleep; I was "slept out." Around 0200 on each of the last three mornings in hack, I quietly snuck up on the flight-deck catwalk and prowled around to get some fresh air and a little exercise.

Finally, the rugged shake-down cruise was over and all the air group pilots were carrier qualified without any pilot fatalities. The seas were rough as the *Hornet* proceeded north near Cape Hatteras. One night the ship must have hit a rogue wave and the ship shuddered violently. I jumped from my bunk and joined some other nervous pilots in the passage way, one pilot had already donned his aviation life jacket. Nothing more happened that night, but the ship continued to pitch and roll until the sea quieted down the next day. On 31 January, all the flyable aircraft that hadn't been banged up were launched to fly back to Norfolk.

After the ship docked, my roommate and I checked into the Breeze Point officer's quarters. As I was walking toward the quarterdeck with a load of clothes in my arms, I was stopped by our squadron operations officer LT "Moe" Vose. Using the nickname he tagged me with, he said, "Chowder Head," you're going to stay aboard ship for three more days." I asked, "Why me?" After telling him Annie was due back in Norfolk the next day, and I needed to meet her at the train station — a little lie — he just looked at me with his big, brown sorrowful eyes and walked away. The junior pilots in the squadron had tagged him "Woeful Moe."

During the time of our shake-down cruise, Annie had traveled back to her home to spend time with her mother. She had made plans to return to Norfolk after the *Hornet's* return to port. I had to send her a telegram to delay her return trip. To put it mildly, I was devastated, but knew I was a victim of being in the wrong place at the right time when Woeful Moe was looking for a pilot to stay aboard.

Later, I found out why I was ordered to stay aboard. The *Hornet* was going to trial launch two Army *B-25* bombers off her flight deck, and they wanted a Navy carrier pilot to hob-knob with the Army *B-25* pilots in our ready room. We talked about carrier takeoffs, and I shared my experience of my first takeoff. I told them, "It's a scary feeling because you feel like you're going way too slow to get airborne." I explained some simple arithmetic, "If the ship is traveling at 23 knots, and the prevailing wind is 16 knots, then there is a 39-knots component of wind flowing over your wings while your plane is stationary. And because the *B-25* needs 85 knots to get airborne, you will only need 46 knots going down the flight to get airborne. Take a quick glimpse at the water instead of the planks on the flight deck as you roll down the deck, and you will sense your actual airspeed over the water." The *B-25* lifted off successfully — better than our Navy planes — but didn't create much interest or attention. History would be made on 18 April 1942, when the *Hornet* would launch fifteen *B-25s* for a bombing raid on Tokyo.

After Annie returned to Norfolk, we planned to get married even though we knew the war could rip our lives apart. We sensed if we didn't tie the knot now, we would probably never marry. We were running out of time because the *Hornet* would be deploying some time in the near future. All ships movements were highly classified in those days, so the crew was kept in the dark of when and where.

On the morning of 10 February, I was awakened about 0400 by our squadron duty officer who handed me a telegram telling me my father had died from a heart attack. The squadron commander was reluctant to grant me emergency leave, but finally allowed me seven days leave telling me that I could be called back at any time if the ship was going to deploy.

Annie managed to reserve a seat for me on an Eastern Airlines flight to Chicago, and I arrived by train to my home in Janesville around midnight. This time I got the royal reception from my dog, Peter. He kept jumping up to lick my face, and I rolled on the floor with him. He knew his old buddy this time. The funeral service was a very emotional time, especially when I saw the pair of miniature Navy gold wings I'd given my dad pinned on his suit lapel. It was a difficult time for my mother, and she collapsed in my arms as she viewed my father for the last time.

HOOKED

The next day I told my mother that Annie and I hoped to be married in Norfolk before the *Hornet* deployed to an unknown destination. I was concerned how she would feel about my marriage plans so soon after my father's funeral; however, she told she understood the situation and helped me select a wedding band.

Two days later, after a travel ordeal by train back to Norfolk, Annie and I spent most of a day getting a Virginia vehicle license. Before Congress passed the *Soldiers and Sailors Relief Act*, servicemen in Virginia had to obtain state automobile license tags even if they lived on the base and had a valid license from another state. The Norfolk police had arrested Navy personnel driving off the air station without valid auto licenses. This was unfair, considering the necessary deployments and moves of servicemen.

We had originally planned to be married in the Navy Chapel on the air station, but the state of Virginia required blood tests and a three-day wait before you could obtain a marriage license. Ensign Louis Muery, a friend and squadron pilot, told me we could get married in North Carolina without blood tests. The nearest Justice of the Peace was in South Mills, North Carolina, and Louis and his fiancée, offered to accompany us to South Mills to be witnesses. We located the blurry-eyed Justice of the Peace, and the ceremony was so brief, we questioned if we were really married. The old saying *"Marry in haste, and repent in leisure,"* never applied to our marriage. That night, 18 February 1942, was the beginning of sixty-six years together, and we are still counting.

When Annie worked at Doctor's Hospital in Washington D.C., she rode horse's English style, decked out in a riding habit wearing a snazzy brown derby. One day, she coaxed me into riding with her at Virginia Beach. I had never ridden anything but a pony, and I couldn't get my horse to move. It just stood still. I needed a throttle. So we traded horses. Same result. How humiliating — a fearless dive-bomber pilot — and I couldn't even bully a horse to move.

Ensign KB White, my *Hornet* roommate, visited our apartment as we were approaching deployment time, and when he spotted the brown derby and the riding crop, he just sort of appropriated them. Aboard the *Hornet,* he loved wearing the derby especially when he played his saxophone. With the derby pulled down over his eyes and his feet propped up on the desk, he'd fill our room with sweet sentimental music. The derby was lost 26 October, 1942 with the sinking of the *Hornet.* In a letter from KB dated 23 January 1997:

> *"When Annie's derby was modeled by several* VB-8 *pilots in our ready room, the hilarious results were very stimulating to our morale - not everybody looks dashing in a derby. Annie, I promise to return it forthwith as soon as I recover it."*

During the war, the Army had positioned large searchlight units in the Norfolk vicinity. One night, after finishing a training flight, I was circling above the air station and Willoughby Bay at 1,000 feet when a searchlight spotted me and zeroed in. The light reflected off my wings and lit up the interior of my cockpit. The Army boys wanted to play. I decided to accommodate them and climbed up to 5,000 feet as more search lights lit up and locked on me. To avoid the lights, I switched off the planes exterior lights and rolled into a steep dive for a couple thousand feet. As soon as I lost the lights, I would climb again to regain altitude, and the searchlight would pick me up. It was an action-packed game that afforded the Army crews some darn good training and a sideshow for the folks on the ground.

On 4 March, Annie had picked up groceries and drove to the dock to pick me up for dinner. She was stunned; the *Hornet's* berth was empty. With little warning, the Hornet had departed Norfolk and was now en route to join the Pacific Fleet.

CHAPTER 5
HORNET DEPLOYMENT
TO PACIFIC FLEET

T he *Hornet* and some destroyers rendezvoused a few miles off the Atlantic coast with a task force, which included troop ships. We were to accompany the troop ships as far as the Panama Canal. The *Hornet* would then head to San Diego to join the Pacific Fleet, and the troop ships to Australia.

The sea off Cape Hatteras lived up to its reputation with strong winds and very rough high seas. Seasickness was probably the order of the day for many of the Army troops. The *Hornet* dive-bomber pilots flew continuous daylight anti-submarine patrols around the perimeter of the task force. Each plane carried a 600-pound, anti-submarine depth charge. No German submarine periscopes were ever sighted.

While flying a two hour anti-submarine patrol, I watched the *Hornet* pitching wildly and wallowing in the heavy seas. The stern was not only pitching up and down but also rotating in an elliptical pattern. All of my accumulated 35 carrier landings during our shakedown cruise were in the Gulf of Mexico's smooth waters. This landing attempt was going to be a new challenge for me and for the LSO's abilities. The LSO would try to time the pitch of the flight deck, so when the deck was at the midpoint of the pitch cycle and the deck was just starting to go down, the LSO could give the cut signal for the plane to land. There were two dangerous situations, the plane hitting the flight deck ramp or the plane being so high its tail hook had no chance of catching an arresting gear wire resulting in the plane clearing the safety barrier and crashing into the planes parked up the flight deck.

After watching the *Hornet's* gyrations for the two hours, I wondered how our squadron chief petty officer was faring in my rear seat. Looking in my rear view mirror, I saw that he was staring intensely down at the *Hornet*. If he wasn't worried, he should have been, considering my scant carrier landing experience.

While watching the *Hornet* swing into the wind to recover aircraft, my adrenaline kicked in — a good sign in this situation. Turning into my final approach, I saw the LSO's signals. He was giving me a roger, which meant that my speed and altitude were correct, and the deck was almost level as I received a cut. Then, the deck dropped away just as the plane's nose dipped down. Immediately, I pulled back hard on the control stick to level the plane as the flight deck was coming back up and my wheels hit the flight deck with a hard thud. The old *Curtiss* dive bomber had a very strong landing gear and soft shock absorbers, which prevented the landing gear from collapsing. I was still shaking when I walked into the squadron's ready room. That would be the worst sea condition I would ever encounter during my carrier deployments.

Calm seas greeted us in the Caribbean, but the word got around that the Caribbean was teeming with sharks. I questioned again why I was flying for the Navy when I could have flown for the Army Air Corps.

Before entering the Panama Canal, we flew our planes off the *Hornet* and landed them at Howard Field. As we reached landfall, we had to fly over dark-green, soupy and sinister looking swamps. Howard Field had a single landing strip with a small mountain near the approach end of the strip. The Army pilots made straight-in landing approaches, dipping down after clearing the mountain and then touched down. Not the Navy pilots. We "peeled off" from our formation, turned downwind doing a tight 180-degree turn inside of the mountain and lined up with the runway.

As I was starting to roll out of a tight left turn to line up with the runway, I must have hit an updraft from the wind hitting the base of the mountain. My plane started to roll out of control to the left; the wings were almost vertical to the runway. Just as I got my wings leveled, the wheels hit the runway. Even though I was aware that the wind turbulence from the mountain almost crashed my plane, ultimately, I rationalized that I had let my air speed get too slow in the final stages of landing. This mindset was going to cause me trouble when I prepared to land back aboard the *Hornet* on the Pacific side of the Canal.

Squadron Fiasco

The next morning, our squadron was ordered to fly over to Albrook Field, another Army field that was just a couple miles on the same longitudinal line from Howard Field. Our squadron commander briefed us and told us to take off in a line and land in the same direction as we had taken off at Howard Field. Our leader assumed the wind direction would be the same at both fields. After I had touched down on the runway, I saw two planes ahead of me swerving back and forth before taxiing off the runway. After landing, my plane started swerving, and I stomped hard alternately on each brake to stay on the runway. As I taxied off the runway, I couldn't believe the carnage behind me. Three planes had ground looped, swerving around in a circle, and one plane tore a lower wing panel off. What had caused this fiasco was that we had all landed downwind!

A very angry air operations officer, an Army lieutenant colonel, viewed the wreckage cluttering his field and just shook his head. This was an embarrassing incident for a Navy squadron to screw up on an Army field. The next morning, adding insult to injury, as we taxied out to the runway, one of the plane's landing gear collapsed. That now left four wrecked Navy planes at Albrook Field.

In 1944, there was to be a sequel to this incident at an Army air base in Birmingham, Alabama. As a flight leader, I had volunteered to lead the flight to ferry eight Brewster *SB2A Buccaneer* dive bombers from the Vero Beach naval air station to the Memphis naval air station. Our flight landed at the Maxwell Army air base in Montgomery, Alabama, to refuel, but the base operations officer would not let us refuel until after a scheduled air show. The Navy prohibited ferrying aircraft at night, and this delay would prevent us from reaching Memphis before dark. I decided to fly to the Army air base at Birmingham, Alabama to refuel. That was a big mistake. When I filed a flight plan, the operations officer never told me the air base was closed to transient aircraft because the *B-29* bomber aircraft located there were being outfitted with secret modifications. In addition, I had failed to a read a "Notam," a notice to airmen restricting transient planes from landing at the Birmingham base.

As we approached the air base, my radio quit functioning. I turned the flight lead over to my wingman, so he could get our landing instructions. The weather was deteriorating. We were already flying under an overcast that created a 1,500 foot ceiling, and the low mountain ridge near the field reduced it down to 500 feet. We all had about thirty minutes of fuel left. Our new flight leader kept circling the base. I was waiting for him to break off from our formation, so we could land. Finally, he broke off and started to land on the active runway and immediately received a red light from the control tower. After some of our planes received the red light, the pilots had to abort their landings. With little remaining fuel, pilots were desperate, and — rules be damned — they all commenced landing against the red light. The control tower finally gave the green light, and I followed the last plane in. One pilot landed on a different runway, but found the runway littered with tires, fifty-gallon oil drums and planks. It was a closed runway. Miraculously, he didn't hit any of the larger debris, but did blow a tire.

It was a relief with the planes safely on the ground. I wasn't too concerned when the base operations officer, a lieutenant colonel, started chewing me out until, to my chagrin, I recognized him as the same lieutenant colonel from Albrook. And he verified it when he said, "This is the biggest fiasco I've had with Navy planes since the one I had in Panama." Looking at him rather sheepishly, I said, "Colonel, I was there," and we both grinned and shook hands.

After leaving Albrook Field to land back on the *Hornet* in the Pacific, I was treated to an amazing sight. The sea was dead calm, except for large rings and smaller rings in the water created by big fish attacking smaller fish and those fish attacking even smaller fish, at least that's what it looked like from my vantage point.

For planes to land on the *Hornet* with no wind, the ship would have to be at almost maximum speed to get sufficient wind across her flight deck. All the planes would be landing "hotter." When it was my turn to land, I kept my air speed a little too high because of my hairy landing episode at Howard Field. The LSO gave me the "slightly fast" signal a couple of times in my approach, but still gave me the cut signal. My tailhook caught a wire, and the plane shuddered violently. At first I thought my landing gear had collapsed, but the plane was still moving forward and angling toward the port side of the flight deck. By kicking in the right rudder hard and jamming the throttle full forward, I attempted to keep the plane from sliding backwards off the flight deck. I succeeded, and the plane ended up resting on the flight deck with the engine facing the ship's island. I noticed crew members standing on the island catwalk laughing and pointing back down the flight deck. What was so funny? My tailhook, tail wheel and pieces of metal from the tail assembly laid all twisted up in the arresting wire. This was too good to pass up; a squadron pilot drew a cartoon of a tailhook representing a feathered arrow shooting off the stern by a landing arresting wire with the caption: "The *Hornet* gets its first piece of tail."

Because the tail assembly had failed, an inspection on all the dive bombers revealed loose rivets in the tail assembly. Back in Norfolk, our planes had armored pilot's seats and self-sealing gas tanks installed. These tanks prevented incendiary bullets from setting fuel on fire. All this added weight to the plane changed its flight characteristics, causing the plane's nose to pass beyond ninety degrees during dive-bombing and also making the dive slightly upside down. And because of this, it took a lot more stick pressure control to recover from a dive. All the planes were declared unsafe for carrier landings, and would never fly off the *Hornet* again.

HOOKED

Burial at Sea
15 March

"Beneath a sky of unbelievably light blue, we have just experienced our first funeral at sea. While smallish clouds of white cotton hung motionless in the sky, overhead as all hands stood quietly with a rigidity that is not discipline but an act of respect. The ceremonies on the hanger deck were a token of the conclusion to a life spent in the service of this country, given while on duty at sea. Today there is newness to the ritual, which with the passage of time in these waters will wear off without dimming the solemnity of the occasion. Four destroyers, two heavy cruisers and an aircraft carrier flew their ensigns at half-mast in tribute to one reserve apprentice seaman, symbolizing as effectively as anything does I have yet seen the tangible evidence that this nation holds the life of even the lowliest as worthy of tribute as the mighty. It is fitting that men and officer's stand quietly in that sun until taps are sounded and the shrouded body is lowered into the sea."

Ensign Bill Evans, a Torpedo Squadron Eight pilot, wrote the above description. He would later be shot down and killed during the Battle of Midway. I found the roughly typed narrative when I helped inventory Evan's personal effects and made a copy. It needed considerable editing, but, to me, it was a beautiful description of that solemn day.

CHAPTER 6
SAN DIEGO AND SAN FRANCISCO

The Douglas Dauntless SBD Dive-Bomber

The *Hornet* arrived in San Diego about the middle of March and docked at the North Island air station. The dive-bomber squadrons were assigned *SBD-3* Douglas *Dauntless* dive-bombers. These planes were all "used" but serviceable. On 25 March, in the *SBD*, I was going to have my first practice landings at Brown Field, a Navy field located near the Mexican border. Sitting in the rear seat, a squadron pilot with *SBD* flying experience flew me to Brown Field to demonstrate the plane's landing characteristics. But, when we arrived over the field, two *SBDs* had crashed on the runway while landing. The *SBD* being a monoplane was tricky, if you got too slow when flaring out to land, a wing could stall out, flip down and hit the runway. We couldn't land, so we flew back to the air station. We later learned one pilot had been killed. The other pilot lost an eye and later was medically discharged from the Navy. In the next three days, I only logged eight familiarization flight hours in the *SBD*. All our squadron pilots badly needed FCLP and dive-bombing practice in the *SBD*. My next flight in a *SB*D would not be until 27 April at Ford Island Airfield at Pearl Harbor.

Navy Wives Chasing the Ship

Even though ships movements were highly classified, Navy wives knew the *Hornet* was headed for San Diego. Annie, and a squadron lieutenant's wife, Judy Ellenberg, and her baby were driving from Norfolk to San Diego. While en route in east Texas on a rainy day,

Judy's car entered a curve covered with slick mud that had washed on the road. The car skidded out of control and rolled over as it went down an embankment. Annie was thrown clear from the car and suffered multiple bruises. Fortunately, there were no serious injuries. People in the car following behind them witnessed the accident, assisted getting the girls and baby back up to the road and then drove them to the nearest town for medical assistance. Judy's auto insurance company representatives took over and arranged for rail travel from Dallas to San Diego. Annie, Judy and the baby finally arrived at the San Diego rail depot at noon on a Sunday, probably the last week of March.

LT Ellenberg and I met Judy and Annie at the San Diego railroad station when their train arrived at 1200, and we took them to the Hotel del Coronado in Coronado, across the bay from San Diego. After Annie and Judy's long cross-country trek, it would be a short rendezvous of only eight hours. Sadly, the wives received the heartbreaking news that all *Hornet* personnel had to report aboard the Hornet at 2000 that night. This was a traumatic experience for a bride of two months. After seeing how badly bruised Annie was from the car accident, it seemed unbelievable she had not been more seriously injured.

The next morning, the *Hornet* departed from San Diego heading for San Francisco. The next afternoon, it was a beautiful clear day as we approached the entrance to the San Francisco Bay. The sun was reflecting off the white homes on the western hills sloping down toward the ocean. It was an impressive sight, looking up at the Golden Gate Bridge as we sailed beneath it; an experience I've never forgotten.

As the *Hornet* approached the Alameda air station dock, a number of *B-25* twin-engine bombers were parked on the dock, and it was obvious the *B-25s* would be loaded onto the *Hornet's* flight deck. To make room, all the *Hornet's* aircraft had been jammed on the hanger deck. The speculation was that the *B-25s* were being ferried to some unknown destination. More *B-25s* were landing at the air station and I watched a *B-25* fly under the Golden Gate Bridge. Flying under the bridge was probably prohibited, but as Navy pilots, we admired the *B-25* pilot's daring exploit.

Late in the evening, on the same day after the *Hornet* left San Diego, the word got out that the ship had gone to San Francisco and would dock at Alameda Naval Air Station. Although the Hornet was five-hundred miles away, the temptation to see their husbands one last time before they departed to sea caused the wives to do what was known as "chasing the ship." Annie and three other young brides dumped their suitcases in a car and caught the last night ferry from Coronado across the bay to San Diego. The girls drove all night and arrived in San Francisco the next afternoon, knowing their husbands would be in for an unexpected surprise.

The *Hornet* would be in port for only two days, and in wartime, the Navy allowed only half the officers and crewmen to go on "liberty" each night. The *Hornet's* personnel were divided into two groups called "starboard" and "port." I was in the starboard group that could go on liberty the first night. A small group of our squadron's pilots and I spent the evening at the *Top of the Mark,* a restaurant and bar at the Mark Hopkins Hotel. A young medical doctor, who was about to enter the Naval Medical Corp, and his wife joined our group. He was excited about meeting and talking with naval aviators and generously paid for our drinks. Later, he hosted our group at the Palace Hotel for a late dinner. As pay back, we enthusiastically took turns dancing with his lovely wife. At the end of the evening, they invited us to an Easter dinner at their home in Santa Cruz. We thanked him but said the Navy had other plans for us.

The next night, I expected to spend a dull evening aboard the *Hornet.* As I was walking by the squadron office, our executive office was chastising one of our pilots and emphatically said, "TJ", you're not going on liberty." I didn't know why TJ, one of our pilots, was being punished, but I quickly asked, "Can I go in his place?" The answer was, "Sure." I was the only pilot in our squadron to go on liberty both nights, and I was to find out it would be serendipity at its best.

As the liberty boat approached the dock at the *Embarcadero* in San

Francisco, an officer standing near the bow of boat said, "Look at those two "chippies" on the dock. As the boat got closer to the dock, I blurted out, "Hell, they're not chippies; one is my wife!" I was happily stunned, and Annie and I wasted no time checking into the Claremont Hotel that night. The other girl standing on the dock with Annie didn't find her husband, and sadly her husband, a pilot in the *Hornet's* torpedo squadron was shot down and killed 4 June in the Battle of Midway. Liberty was up at 0800 the next morning, so I caught the 0600 liberty boat back to the *Hornet*. Everyone in the boat was quiet and subdued, lost in their own thoughts.

As the *Hornet* passed under the *Golden Gate,* I felt melancholy; it was like the ending of a play with the curtain coming down. Would I ever see San Francisco and the bridge again? More importantly, would I ever see Annie again? What did destiny have in store for me? Luck was my companion. Although being wounded and having to ditch in the sea, I would survive two major carrier battles. After the *Hornet* was well out to sea, a Navy blimp dropped a message bag on her flight deck, and the speculation about the *B-25s* was over. The *B-25s* were going to fly off the *Hornet* and bomb Tokyo.

CHAPTER 7
THE B-25 MISSION TO BOMB TOKYO
18 APRIL 1942

Led by Colonel Jimmie Doolittle

With all our planes stowed in the hanger deck, the *Hornet* pilots had nothing to do but eat, sleep and play cards. Just getting a haircut was an event. Some of our experienced Navy gamblers, mostly bachelors, won most of the *B-25* pilot's money, but returned all their winnings to them before they flew off the *Hornet*. In addition, they gave them cartons of cigarettes. Nobody worried about cigarettes being detrimental to your health during that wartime era. The *B-25* pilots ate in the officer's wardroom, but most of us didn't get many opportunities to mingle and talk with them. When I did, I found they were more apprehensive about flying their *B-25s* off the *Hornet's* deck, than their upcoming bombing mission. We did get to observe the *B-25* pilots while they were eating in our wardroom. One of the *B-25* pilots sitting at our table across from me would end up being captured in China, taken to Japan and then executed by being beheaded.

The *Hornet* and our escort ships rendezvoused with the *USS Enterprise* along with her escort ships which had been deployed from Pearl Harbor five days after we left San Francisco. The *Enterprise's* dive bombers flew searches ahead of the task force while the *Hornet* approached a planned launch point for the *B-25s* which was about 450 miles from Tokyo. The launch point was within the search range of Japanese patrol planes. With sea conditions deteriorating, the escorting destroyers had to be left behind for the final run into the launch position.

HOOKED

On 18 April, *Enterprise* search planes spotted two Japanese fishing trollers, boats that were radio equipped to serve as pickets to guard Japanese waters. Warning radio messages from these picket boats were being monitored by our ships. The boats were about 650 miles from Tokyo and had to be immediately destroyed. The *Enterprise* search planes strafed and attempted to bomb the boats, but they weren't sinking fast enough and a destroyer finally sunk both boats with shellfire but not before the radio messages had been sent. The *Hornet* passed some debris containing a body. Seeing this gruesome sight made the war seem very real.

The task force commander ordered the *B-25* pilots and crews to prepare to launch. The new unexpected launch location was over 600 miles away from the designated airfields in China, too far for the *B-25's* to reach even using the additional cans of fuel secured inside each plane to extend their flight range. This meant the flight crews would either parachute over China or crash-land their planes. The sea conditions were bad and the *Hornet* was pitching heavily. I watched the takeoffs from the *Hornet's* starboard catwalk.

Hornet pitching in rough seas, ready to launch – B-25s - U.S. Navy photo

THE B-25 MISSION TO BOMB TOKYO

Colonel Jimmie Doolittle's plane was the first to takeoff as the bow of the flight deck was leveling toward center. His plane lifted with ease and as he gained altitude in a climbing turn, he finally leveled off and headed for Tokyo. From my position on the catwalk, I could see the white expressionless faces of the co-pilots as each plane was lifting off the flight deck. One pilot pulled the plane's nose up too soon, and the plane was dragging it's tailskid on the deck. The plane ballooned sharply up and seemed to hang in the air, and I thought the plane was going to drop a wing and spin in. The ship's bow was coming up, and the plane disappeared from sight. As the bow dropped down, the plane became visible, just skimming the waves with propellers blowing mists of seawater in the air.

First B-25 launched from Hornet - U.S Navy photo

The *Hornet's* plane director, signaling pilots for takeoffs, was having trouble staying on his feet as the strong wind whipped across the slippery deck. He was blown into a propeller and lost an arm at his shoulder. Even at my observation post, I was getting doused from the seawater spraying down the deck each time the bow dipped low and hit a big wave.

B-25 launched from USS Hornet - B-25s are visible on flight deck
U.S. Navy photo

As the day proceeded into evening, Japanese radio stations were being closely monitored for information about the Japanese reactions to the bombing attack. As soon as the *B-25s* were launched, the task force high-tailed east to get out of range of the Japanese long-range bombers. The *Hornet's* fighter aircraft were quickly brought up to the flight deck and readied for flight operations. Our destroyers which had been left behind were finally sighted and rejoined the task force as we headed for Pearl Harbor.

All the outgoing personal mail from the *Hornet* was censored. I wrote a letter to Annie after we reached Pearl Harbor and mentioned the date of our wedding, 18 February, as being an important day in our lives. She found an old newspaper dated 18 April with the story about the bombing of Tokyo. She connected the dots and knew the *Hornet* had launched the bombers.

Return to Pearl Harbor

The dive bomber's secondary mission was scouting ahead of the task forces searching for enemy ships. Before the war, it was my understanding carrier planes didn't fly singly over fifty miles from the carriers. Now, dive-bomber pilots would fly 200-mile single-plane searches every day that the *Hornet* was at sea. A short-range-radio homing device called a "ZB" had a radio signal which could only be received on a "line of sight" from radio receivers installed in our carrier aircraft. The carrier's transmitter was called "YE." The transmitting signal covered a 360-degree area by a rotating antenna. The 360-degree area was divided into 20-degree sectors and each sector was assigned a Morse code letter. When you identified the sector letter, you could correct your course to the ship. The ZB was invaluable; a functioning radio was our lifeline to the ship.

LT Randall, who was flying our squadron's first 200-mile search, was overdue. Although his plane was picked up on the *Hornet's* radar screen, the task force operating under the doctrine of "radio silence" was prohibited from giving LT Randall his course and distance to the ship. Finally, the radar blip disappeared from the screen. LT Randall became our squadron's first casualty. He was married, and Annie and I remembered seeing the lieutenant and his blond wife at a Saturday night formal party back at the Norfolk Air Station's Officers Club. They were the life of the party. She wore a bright-red evening gown, and he was attired in formal dress with tails. They both were accomplished dancers and Gardner's long tails were really flying around that evening.

As the *Hornet* was entering the channel to Pearl Harbor on 26 April, we observed some of the after-effects of the Japanese air attack on that fateful Sunday morning of 7 December. Black oil coated the harbor's channel banks and the beach areas. The battleship *USS Arizona's* wrecked bridge structure was visible above water. Attached to a capsized battle ship were large cables anchored on the beach in preparations to right it. The battleship, the *USS California*, was being repaired in a dry dock, and most of the other dock areas had been cleared of wreckage and were usable.

On 27 April, it had been a month since I flew my first flight in a *SBD* dive bomber. All our pilots badly needed FCLP (field carrier landing practice) and dive-bombing practice on target boats at sea. The turbulent winds terminated all FCLP because it was too dangerous to slow the planes down in the final approach pattern. I had only flown three flights and logged all of four hours. The *Hornet* was to deploy 30 April to the South Pacific, and I would make my first carrier landing in the *SBD*. All I knew was that in slowing the air speed of the *SBD* for a carrier landing, the plane would stall out at about 75 knots.

CHAPTER 8
DEPLOYMENT TO SOUTH PACIFIC

The *Hornet* was fifty miles at sea. I was about half way from Pearl Harbor and the ship when my engine backfired and started to quit. I immediately shifted to my No. 2 main fuel tank, and the engine restarted. I suspected there was water in the first tank. A few minutes later the engine quit again. The *SBD* had two smaller auxiliary tanks, and I switched to an auxiliary tank. Again, the engine restarted, and after a few minutes, the engine quit a second time. After switching to my last auxiliary tank, the engine started, backfired and kept running — but for how long? Finally, I made it inside the destroyer screen around the task force, which was a relief knowing if I had to ditch, I'd be rescued. Not knowing how little fuel was left in that small auxiliary tank, I needed to land on my first approach. My first attempt was successful and anti-climatic after my near ditching.

The aviation fuel tanks on aircraft carriers are topped off with water to eliminate volatile fumes. The fuel for aircraft is pumped from the top of the carrier's tanks, and there had been a couple of previous incidents where water had seeped into the aircraft fuel tanks. I think the reason I didn't have water in my second auxiliary tank was that the tank was still full of gas after the plane's last flight.

Everyday, during a deployment, the *SBD* squadrons flew 200-mile single plane searches to cover 180 degrees ahead of the task force. Each plane covered a 20-degree sector. Just before dawn, the first search of nine aircraft launched, and in the afternoon, about four hours before dusk, another search group launched. The searches averaged about three and half hours, and each plane carried a 600-pound depth charge to use against enemy submarines. The ships and aircraft operated under the doctrine of radio silence. If a search plane had engine failure beyond radar range, the prospects of rescue were dim as the search area would be huge. We navigated by dead-reckoning, a time and distance problem. Our out leg was 200 miles, a twenty mile cross leg and about 220 miles back to the *Hornet*. For our navigation problems, we used a *fictitious ship*. The *Hornet* could be moving about fifty miles during the time of the searches but was supposed to be at the fictitious position when the searches were completed, we hoped. We flew low, at about 500 feet, so we could judge wind direction and velocity by watching the white caps. When white caps break, the scud moves back into the direction of the wind; the size of the white caps indicates the wind velocity. We recorded any notable changes of wind and direction on our navigation plotting boards which slid into tracks under the instrument panel when not in use. On the return navigation leg we could, if needed, make course changes to our in-bound leg.

The *Hornet* had a wind direction and velocity indicator mounted near the bow. By watching the white caps, you could estimate the direction and velocity of the wind and verify your estimate from the indicator readings. We used a buddy system to work out our individual navigation problem with another squadron pilot. The data was recorded on work sheets and then was compared to eliminate errors. In addition, copies of the work sheets were checked for errors by a ship's navigation officer.

On one search, I passed over the *Hornet* at the exact time my search was supposed to end — perfect navigation. I bragged to the pilots in our ready room saying, "I flew a perfect search and must have homing-pigeon blood." Somebody said, "Fisher, sit down and shut up, the *Hornet* is fifty miles from our *fictitious ship's* position!" On another search, the sea was dead calm, no wind, and there was unlimited visibility. I ended my search with no ships in sight. My radioman hadn't been able to pick up a signal on our ZB. I decided to continue on course for another five minutes and still no ships. Now I was concerned and climbed up to 3,000 feet and continued on the same course for another five minutes, still no ships in sight. Now I felt desperate and scared. What should I do next? I decided to fly an additional five minutes and, finally, spotted the tiny white wake of a destroyer. I never could figure out the huge error in my navigation.

On another search after flying fifteen minutes out the first leg, I had a rude awakening. I should have been flying a course of 330-degrees, but I was flying 300-degrees! After immediately returning to the Hornet, I resumed my correct search course of 330 degrees. Now I had to correct my navigation problem for the fifteen minutes I had lost. My radioman monitored the course and altitude of the plane while I reworked my navigation. It was a dangerous thing to do. I should have aborted the search and just circled the task force until the *Hornet* recovered the other search planes.

Crossing the Equator- Shellbacks and Pollywogs

In the U.S. Navy when a ship crosses the equator, a time-honored traditional ceremony takes place. Crew men who had previously crossed the equator were called "Shellbacks," and they planned and organized the event. "Pollywogs" were crew members who had never crossed the equator. They would be inducted into the *"Mysteries of the Deep"* by Neptunus Rex and his Royal court. Some of the principal members of the Royal party were Davy Jones, Neptune's first assistant; Her Highness Amphitrite, Goddess of the Sea; and the Royal Baby.

The Royal family dressed in costumes and perched on a platform near the stern of the ship. Other Shellbacks dressed in pirate costumes. The Royal Baby — always a large sailor with a good-size paunch — had his belly smeared with vile stuff, and all Pollywogs had to pay homage by kissing the Royal Baby's greasy belly. Besides that repulsive act, the Shellbacks concocted other traditional unpleasant activities for the Pollywogs initiation into the royal court. One event was particularly harsh. They swatted the Pollywogs with sailor's belts as they ran down a belt line. Waiting my turn, I noticed officers ahead of me were being hit hard with the buckle end of the belts. The situation was getting out of hand. A senior ship's officer yelled, "No more officers!" Thankfully, my initiation was over. King Neptune signed my card, and I became a certified Shellback.

The day before the Hornet crossed the equator, I had already flown across the equator 175 hundred miles ahead of the *Hornet* while flying a 200-mile search. I had plotted in the point on my navigation board and the time I would fly across the equators line. I planned to strafe the equator's line after charging the two 50-caliber guns that were synchronized to fire between the propeller blades, but suddenly hesitated. I was out 175 miles ahead of the *Hornet,* and if the synchronizing system failed, I would have literally shot myself down. With trepidation, I fired a short burst and watched the welcome splashes as the bullets hit the water. Back aboard the *Hornet,* I tried to plead my case that I was already a Shellback, but I lost. There was no appeal. I had to cross the equator aboard a ship.

On 8 May 1942, the Battle of Coral Sea was fought in the South Pacific. It was the first battle in history where opposing ships were never in sight of each other. The *USS Lexington* and the *USS Yorktown* were opposed by the two large Japanese carriers, the *Shokaku, Zuikaku,* and the small carrier, *Shoho.* The *Lexington* was sunk and the *Yorktown* suffered serious battle damage. The *Shokaku* also suffered serious battle damage, and the *Soho* was torpedoed and sunk. This was an indication of how vulnerable American and Japanese carriers were without armored flight decks in comparison to the British aircraft carriers with their armored flight decks.

A few days after the Coral Sea battle, our task force, with both the Hornet and the Enterprise, abruptly left the Coral Sea and headed back to Pearl Harbor. This was a mystery and caused a lot of speculation especially among the pilots. Before the task force reached Pearl Harbor, all our air group pilots attended a meeting in the officer's wardroom. We were told the Japanese were going to attack and occupy Midway Island about 4 June. Then the shocker — it was expected the Japanese carrier task force would include five or six of their large carriers! The wardroom was very quiet as the pilots digested this sobering news. We only had the *Hornet* and *Enterprise.* The *Yorktown* had already reached Pearl Harbor and would need three months in dry dock to repair her battle damage. We had just lost the *Lexington* and almost lost the *Yorktown*. The odds seemed almost overwhelming. We could lose both the *Hornet* and *Enterprise*. We were a very somber group of pilots as we filed out of that room. My roommate, KB White, and I sat in our room quietly talking about our slim chances of surviving the looming battle. He showed me an old newspaper picture of one of the Japanese carriers, the *Akagi*. It was a strange-looking ship compared to the *Hornet*. It was tough to carry on with your normal duties and routines, but somehow you had to quit dwelling on what might happen.

CHAPTER 9
RETURN TO PEARL HARBOR

W hile the *Hornet* was returning to Pearl Harbor, Ensign Muery, who had stood up for Annie and me at our wedding, failed to return from an afternoon 200-mile search. As I watched the sun going down, I wondered what had happened to Muery. Had he successfully ditched? Had he and his radioman managed to get in their life raft? The nearest islands were over 200 miles away and some of them were occupied by the Japanese. Due to the urgency for the carriers return to Pearl Harbor, there wasn't any time to conduct a search for Muery.

After the Battle of Midway, when the *Hornet* returned to Pearl Harbor, we learned Muery had survived 23 days in his life raft. Annie and I would meet Muery again in Vero Beach, Florida, in 1943. He was very bitter that no one had searched for him. Here is the amazing story of how he had managed to survive his terrible ordeal. Louis was interviewed by an Associated Press news reporter at Pearl Harbor. I combined the reporter's interview with information I obtained from my personal interviews with Muery in 1943.

Two on Raft for 23 Days
One of Flyers Drowned in Surf off Island

The survivor and the pilot of the plane forced down was Ensign Louis Muery, 23, of Houston, Texas. The following is his story:

"We were a long way from the carrier when our engine stopped. There were just the two of us, Richter and me. In two minutes, it

was over. I crash landed the plane; we managed to get out of our parachute harnesses and on the wing with our rubber life raft. Then the plane sank.

The raft was inflated by compressed gas from a carbon dioxide bottle. We had two quart canteens of water, a 45-caliber pistol with 21 rounds of ammunition, emergency rations normal for two days, two folding aluminum paddles, an air pump and patching equipment for the raft, a first-aid kit, our rubber life jackets, three pocket knifes, two signal flags, a stainless-steel mirror, a whistle, our watches and my parachute. We didn't have any navigational equipment.

Paddled all Night

We decided to make for an island we had noticed about 30 to 50 miles from the area we had gone down. After paddling all night, we were getting nowhere. Hopeful of rescue, we decided to just sit and wait. By the morning of the third day, we decided rescue was unlikely, and we should try to make land before it was too late. We rigged a sail from a piece of the parachute using a paddle for a mast and the handle of one of the signal flags for a yardarm. The sail was too small to be effective. We made two other sails each larger than the first. The third sail proved to be a good one. We made six to eight knots; we steered with the remaining paddle, working in shifts, which grew shorter as we became weaker. Next, we rationed our food figuring a 40-day period. We had our "banquet" every afternoon, and each of us was allowed a quarter can of concentrated food, four or five malted milk tablets, or one quarter of chocolate.

Signals and Grunts

It rained on the fifth day and then about every other day. We tried using the parachute to catch rain water to drink, but that was a failure. Finally we were successful, using a large absorbent cloth sling from the first-aid kit. We held this in the rain until it became soaked, and we would ring the water out into the first aid kit's box.

We managed to get a cup of water for each of us every other day or so.

We stopped talking to each other after the fifth day and communicated almost entirely by signals and grunts. Talking was tiring and dried out our mouths. The sun was cruelly hot and blistered poor Richter's skin terribly. But he never complained. My skin darker and tougher just became more deeply tanned.

The days passed without sign of a sail or land. Our only companions were the tireless sharks, which swam around the raft and nudged the bright aluminum paddle, which seemed to excite their curiosity. We fired the pistol at them.

The Raft Overturns

On the twelfth day, the raft overturned. After a struggle, we righted it again. The accident cost us the pistol and one canteen of water, two of our three knifes, and most of our food with the exception of three bottles of malted milk tablets. The losses didn't bother us too much; we didn't care much by this time. Once I caught a small fish by using a piece of parachute cloth as a net. We ate the raw fish and it tasted very good. On the twentieth, a dark brown shark about seven feet long found us and remained with us all that night. He persisted in bumping the paddle and finally lunged at the raft. He missed the air chamber but cut a six-inch elliptical hole in the canvas bottom of the raft letting water into a depth of about six inches. At daylight, we thought the shark was gone and decided to turn the raft over and repair the hole with some patching material. We got the raft over and dried the bottom in the sun. Just as we were applying the patch, we saw the same shark swimming around again. The shark dashed for Richter' leg which was hanging over the side of the raft, but he drew his leg up just in time. After splashing on the water to scare off the shark, we righted the raft and climbed back in. Not too soon; the shark was back again and remained with us until we made land.

Sees Land at Last

After 23 days, we lay in a stupor in the bottom of the raft; I finally aroused myself long enough to look around. I thought I saw land in the growing morning light. I shook Richter and pointed shoreward. Neither of us could comprehend it really was land. We finally could see the shore line, and we hugged each other and cried.

The island was surrounded by a coral reef; we could see the swells breaking over the reefs. Neither of us knew or realized the danger of attempting to cross over those reefs. We headed the raft toward the shore. The raft caught in the swells quickly overturned and spilled us out of the raft. We managed to hang onto the raft and right it. Then we paddled out to sea along the shore seeking a better place to land. We headed in again. This time the raft was picked up and hurdled like a chip up in the air. Both of us were thrown clear of the raft. We were wearing our inflated life jackets, but they were not much help in that tremendous surf. Richter and I clung to each other trying to help each other. I knew he was a poor swimmer. A swell dashed us into the reef and knocked us apart. Finally, we were washed into shallow water.

Revival Effort in Vain

I saw Richter lying just behind me in the water. He didn't move. I tried to stand up and fell back into the water. The waves kept washing me in to the beach. Finally, I got on my feet and staggered out to Richter. He was white and limp. I could feel no pulse. Then I dragged him to the beach and tried to do artificial respiration until I passed out. After I revived, I knew Richter was dead.

A coconut near by gave me my first food. I felt a little better and explored a little of the island near the shore. My progress was a series of stumbles and falls. I did not know natives were watching me. They thought I was a Jap and that my paddle was a rifle. I was standing looking out to sea when a voice behind me asked, "Who are you? Do you speak English?" This startled me so much I almost fainted. Turning around I saw a group of natives and a white man. I doubt if I was very coherent. I tried to shake his hand. He soon knew I could speak English. The natives, when they knew I was a friend, were delighted, particularly with the handshake. Nothing would do, but I had to shake hands with each of them. They brought me coconut milk and meat and carried me piggyback to their village. I mended rapidly and before long, I was picked up by the Navy. The natives had buried Richter in their cemetery and made a headstone for his grave."

Secretary of the Navy

Muery was interviewed by the Secretary of the Navy, James Forestall, at a naval base in the South Pacific. The Secretary asked Muery if he needed anything, and he told him he needed money. The Secretary told a naval officer, "See that Muery receives some money." The officer told the Secretary, "He doesn't have his pay accounts; I can't pay him." The Secretary told the officer, "Where do you think Muery's pay accounts are, up his asshole. Pay him!"

Left to right: Ensign Lou Muery - Ensign Joe Auman - Ensign Clayton Fisher and Ensign KB White - San Diego, March 1942

CHAPTER 10
THE BATTLE OF MIDWAY
4 JUNE 1942

Prelude

On 26 May, when the *Hornet* was about fifty miles from Pearl Harbor, all the air-group aircraft were launched, and the dive-bomber squadrons flew their planes into Ewa Field, a Marine air station near Pearl Harbor. All our pilots felt relieved not to be flying those lonely 200-mile searches, to be getting away from the daily shipboard routine, and were looking forward to a two days of recreation. After we landed and were assigned living quarters, we were told all our pilots and air-crew members were restricted to the station. Why were we being restricted? We knew too much about the events of the upcoming Midway battle.

It's hard to describe the mental pressure we were all under at that time. You knew you were going into a battle completely out numbered. It was the unknown future that was so worrisome. How many of us would survive? And now we were going to be deprived of a chance for a little mental relaxation. It just didn't seem fair as you watched the air station personal going off the base on liberty. A few bottles of whiskey were given to the pilots to pacify us that evening. After a few of the pilots became inebriated, they ended up in a semi-friendly fight, wrestling on the lava cinders and having a couple fist fights. No one was seriously hurt, but the next morning, there were some faces with skin abrasions and a couple black eyes. This incident did help relieve the pent up frustration. There were no hard feelings between the pilots the next morning but, rather, an increase in the feeling of camaraderie.

*Hornet proceeding up channel Pearl Harbor,
26 May 1942 - U.S. Navy Photo*

Hornet Docked at Pearl Harbor 26 May - U.S Navy photo

THE BATTLE OF MIDWAY 4 JUNE 1942

On the morning of 28 May, our air group flew back aboard the *Hornet*, and we proceeded to a rendezvoused location called "Point Luck" northeast of Midway. The *Yorktown*, still undergoing repairs at Pearl Harbor, would later join our task force. The stage was being set to ambush the enemy carriers. A key factor in setting the ambush was a stroke of luck. Japanese submarines were late in getting to their positions to patrol a line between the Hawaiian Islands and Midway. Our carriers slipped through the line the day before the submarines had been positioned.

On 1 June, I flew a 200-mile search in a northwest sector and was told it was mandatory that I fly the entire 200 miles. About 160 miles out on my first leg, my engine started to vibrate and shake, and I thought it was going to quit. Gradually it smoothed out. About fifteen minutes later, the engine again vibrated. I reversed my course back to the *Hornet*, but when the engine didn't vibrate again, I turned back to continue my search. On my final inbound leg, the engine vibrated a few more times, and each vibration seemed magnified.

After landing, I told our squadron engineering officer, "I refuse to fly that plane again, and it should be grounded." Our assistant engineering officer piped up and said, "I don't think there's any thing seriously wrong with that engine; I'll fly it the next time it's scheduled." I said to myself, "Good luck kid." He flew the plane the morning of 4 June, the first day of the upcoming battle. He was flying with part of our squadron that landed on Midway Island, and his engine quit about thirty miles from the island. He was later rescued by a *PBY* patrol plane.

The *PBY* long-range patrol aircraft reported the first enemy contacts. The Japanese carrier task force was closing the distance to Midway Island – close enough so their aircraft would be within range to reach and attack Midway. It appeared that 4 June would be the big day.

After early evening squadron meetings for pilot briefings, most of the pilots retired to their rooms. The entire ship was unusually quiet with no one moving through the bluish, dimly lit passageways. I had an eerie feeling that my odds for survival the next morning were minimal, even if we achieved our planned surprise attack. Japanese carriers with their experienced fighter pilots and superior *Zero* fighter plane had great successes shooting down enemy aircraft. From post war accounts, the Japanese pilots confident Midway Island would be an easy target, were partying and playing popular music on their record players. That night, I wrote letters to Annie and my mother and told them I had resigned myself to whatever fate had in store for me. If we lost the battle and I died, I knew our country would eventually defeat the Japanese.

I was worried and just plain scared. Nobody wants to die. There are always fatal aviation operational accidents. The younger pilots usually didn't worry about those accidents; those accidents always happened to other pilots. This evening was totally different. Tomorrow, I could be one of those other pilots.

Morning of 4 June

The *Hornet* personnel were at their battle stations well before dawn, and the squadron pilots were assembled in the ready room — our battle station — with none of the usual banter.

In 1942, our squadrons were assigned non-aviation officers to handle the administrative paper work. Most of these administrative types were usually older businessmen, probably over draft age. Our squadron's administrative officer had been employed by the Sun Oil Company and was a friendly likable person. His first name was Samuel, so, of course, Sam was his nickname. After 1 June with the count down for the big battle looming, you could feel the tension among the pilots, including Sam. He started wearing an aviator's type life jacket all the time and, I suspect, even in his bunk. On the morning of June 4th as I was changing from my uniform into my flight suit, Sam was trying to be super helpful while holding one sleeve of my flight suit, so I could get my arm in the sleeve. Sam was so nervous that his hands were shaking badly as he held my sleeve, which, in turn, was making me more nervous. After the upcoming battle was over and the *Hornet* had returned to Pearl Harbor, Sam departed from our squadron. I guess he must have "un–volunteered" his services to the Navy. We never saw Sam again. Later we discovered "Salty Sam's" life jacket hanging on a hook in our ready room. One of our pilots pulled the lanyards to the CO_2 cartridges to inflate the jacket. Nothing happened. There were no cartridges! Salty Sam would have had a rude awakening in the water if he had abandoned ship.

We all quietly watched the telecast screen mounted in the front of the ready room for enemy contact reports. Finally we received the position report; the enemy carrier task force was bearing 247 degrees at a distance of about 200 miles. Each pilot bent over his navigation plotting board entering in the enemy's position and figuring out the times and distances. The *SBD's* had the longest range and fuel would be no problem, but the torpedo planes carrying their very heavy torpedoes wouldn't be able to make it back to the *Hornet*. The fighter planes didn't have external fuel tanks and also would be very limited in their range.

The *Hornet* would be the first to launch all her available aircraft. A petty officer posted the "deck spot," aircraft positions on flight deck, and I noticed my assigned plane number nine was in the front position of the dive bombers. Normally, I flew the No. 9 position in our nine-plane division. At the last minute that morning, I had been volunteered to fly the left-wing position on the CHAG's (Commander Hornet Air Group's) plane. Another pilot from the scouting squadron was going to fly the right wing position.

The CHAG intended to fly ahead and above our two dive-bomber squadrons to coordinate our attack. I was totally devastated. I wanted to be in my own squadron's formation with all those rapid-firing, twin 30-caliber, rear guns from our eighteen dive bombers protecting our tails. Our little three-plane formation would probably be attacked first by the experienced *Zero* fighter pilots. Our squadron doctrine was to stay in formation as long as possible for mutual protection before starting our dive-bombing runs. The torpedo squadrons had to fan out and break up their formations to make their torpedo runs. This is one reason all of them would later become such sitting ducks for the *Zero* fighters.

HOOKED

The command, "All pilots man your planes," was sounded. We hustled out of the ready room and scrambled up to the flight deck to our planes. As I climbed up on the wing to get in the cockpit, I wondered if these would be my last steps. As I was strapped in my seat by my plane captain and was going over my cockpit check-off list, I heard the command, "Start all engines."

Just after starting my engine, I was surprised to have the *Hornet's* chief photographer climb up on my right wing, stick his head in the cockpit and try to talk to me. As I was all keyed up and nervous, I didn't want to talk.

I could barely hear him over the engine's din and wind blasting from the propellers. He was frantically pointing at something behind my head. Finally, I understood him. My plane had an aerial camera mounted in the belly of the plane, and he wanted to show me where the camera switch was located. He had installed the switch just below my headrest. I had to twist my torso part way around in order to reach the switch.

My plane was selected because I was supposed to be the last plane to dive. Being last would allow the camera to record the bomb damage to an enemy ship as I leveled out from my dive. I should have been reassigned a different plane when I became wingman for the CHAG. Somebody screwed up. The only good thing about carrying the camera was that because of its heavy weight, my plane could only be loaded with a single 500-pound bomb.

My plane would burn a little less fuel than the rest of the *SBDs* carrying the 1,000-pound bombs, and that little edge might become very important. The one salient thing about carrier pilots was their compelling need to conserve fuel because the consequence of running out of gas was a salt-water bath.

THE BATTLE OF MIDWAY 4 JUNE 1942

Hornet flight deck - Battle of Midway, 4 June - 1st launch (White arrow identifies SBD B-9 flown by Ensign Fisher) - U.S. Navy photo

After joining up in formation, we started a slow climb to around 16,000 feet. We used a lot of engine power to climb because of those heavy bombs. We also had to use our oxygen masks, which were of an older vintage than what the fighter pilots used. They were uncomfortable and didn't fit snuggly to our faces. When we reached our altitude, I was collecting ice inside the mask from cold air leaking into the mask mixing with the warmer air from my breath. I was having difficulty breathing and removed my mask periodically to clear the accumulating ice. Wearing a summer flight suit for the mild June weather, I shivered from the cold as the temperature continued dropping at the higher altitudes.

When our formation neared the estimated position of the Japanese carriers, we cleared the lower strata layers of broken clouds, and the visibility was unlimited. So far, there were no enemy carriers with their *Zeros* flying combat, air patrols at 15-20,000 feet over their task force. I kept systematically scanning the sky above and to our right for *Zeros*.

Finally, I noticed a large column of black smoke to the southwest of our position which had to be coming from Midway Island. This column of smoke looked very similar to postwar pictures of the smoke bellowing up from the island. You can see large objects such as a mountain range from over a hundred miles, but our flight position had to be closer than forty miles from the Island for me to able to see that 300 foot high smoke column.

As we continued on our southwest course, we had been ordered to maintain radio silence, until we contacted the enemy. The CHAG gave me a visual hand signal, meaning to form a "scouting line" and then pointed down to our left at our scouting squadron's formation. The purpose of a scouting line was to expand a search to cover more area. All the aircraft would break formation and get in a line abreast with large intervals between each aircraft. This peacetime, relic maneuver would break up our defensive, tactical formation, and if we made contact, it would take time jockeying back to a tight formation. The CHAG continued on course, and we were already near our maximum range to have enough fuel to make it back to the *Hornet.*

I dropped off my wing position and dove down to get close enough to pass on the CHAG's order. Just as I was trying to get near enough to the flight leader's aircraft to get his attention, he began a 180-degree turn and assumed a course heading back to the *Hornet.* It was impossible to carry out the Commander's order. I felt it was my duty to rejoin him. I reversed course to try to locate him, and that was a big mistake. All I could see was empty sky. I was alone and felt very vulnerable. I turned back and tried to join up with the scouting squadron's formation. I'd have to burn excess fuel to join the formation, so I just dogged behind. Finally, I could see the *Hornet* and joined the formation as it did a 360-degree recognition turn.

THE BATTLE OF MIDWAY 4 JUNE 1942

After landing, I met a squadron pilot in our ready room. He was upset and crying. He blurted out, "Fisher, you're the only one who's returned from our squadron. None of the fighter or torpedo pilots have gotten back yet." Later, we found out all the fighter pilots had ditched after running out of fuel. Four pilots were killed ditching, and the others were rescued by *PBY* patrol planes a few days later. All 16 of our torpedo planes were shot down. Ensign Gay was the sole survivor.

Based on Midway, a detachment of our torpedo squadron launched six new-type Grumman *TBF* torpedo bombers, and only one pilot survived. A badly damaged plane, piloted by Ensign Ernest, managed to make it back to Midway Island. Ernest maintained control by using the plane's trim tabs, and crash landed with only one wheel down. He sustained a small facial wound, his rear gunner was killed, and the other gunner was badly wounded.

Enterprise and *Yorktown* Dive-Bombers

The *Enterprise* had launched most of her aircraft after the *Hornet* did that morning. The group commander, CDR McClusky, leading a flight of dive bombers, also had not sighted the enemy carriers when he had reached their estimated position. He had to make a difficult decision as the flight had almost reached the limit of the dive bomber's range, the "point of no return" to the *Enterprise.* He elected to continue on the same course for another few minutes and observed an enemy destroyer moving at a high rate of speed on a northeast heading. At this point, McCluskey made a decision that later was considered a major factor in the outcome of the battle. He concluded the fast moving destroyer was going to join up with the enemy carrier task force, so McClusky lead his flight on the same northeast course and finally spotted three aircraft carriers, the *Akagi, Kaga* and *Soryu.* A fourth carrier, the *Hiryu,* which was partially hidden under some clouds, was not sighted. Miraculously, as McClusky led his flight of dive bombers over the carriers, he was followed by LT Best, commander of Bombing Squadron Six, and there were no *Zeros* in sight at their altitude.

HOOKED

The *Zero* fighters, preoccupied with fighting aircraft launched from Midway and the torpedo planes from our three carriers, had exposed their carriers to our dive bombers. The Japanese had a superior torpedo bomber and a deadly effective torpedo. They feared our torpedo planes more than our dive bombers, unaware of how inferior our torpedo planes and torpedoes were compared to theirs. This major misconception enabled "open season" by our dive bombers on their unprotected carriers.

McCluskey and Best concentrated their attacks on the *Akagi* and *Kagi*. The *Enterprise's* dive bombers obtained multiple direct hits with 500- and 1000-pound bombs on the two carriers. Those bombs destroyed planes on the flight decks, gutted the hanger decks loaded with bombs and torpedoes causing multiple explosions. One dive - bomber was hit by the heavy AA and crashed into the sea.

The *Yorktown's* dive bombers, launched later from a closer range, arrived over the third carrier, the *Soryu,* almost simultaneously with the *Enterprise* dive bombers. Although it wasn't a planned coordinated attack, it was highly successful with Bombing Squadron Five dooming the carrier with three direct hits. The *Soryu* sank about an hour later, a shattering defeat for the enemy.

After a Japanese search plane from the cruiser *Tone* belatedly discovered the presence of the *Yorktown,* enemy carriers were caught in the midst of trying to recover aircraft and rearming and refueling them for a second attack on Midway. Their task force commander, after receiving the stunning news of an enemy task force with at least one aircraft carrier - and probably more - ordered bombers already armed with bombs to be rearmed with torpedoes. This created a catastrophic situation with bombs and torpedoes exposed on the flight and hanger decks. When the bombs from our dive bombers exploded on the flight and hanger decks they caused exposed bombs and torpedoes to detonate. Both carriers were so badly damaged they sank that evening.

The description of the explosions and fires could only be described as it was in Dante's *Inferno.* The book *Shattered Sword, The Untold*

THE BATTLE OF MIDWAY 4 JUNE 1942

Story of The Battle of Midway by Jonathan B, Pashall and Anthony P.Tully contains vivid accounts by Japanese survivors, who were aboard the Japanese aircraft carriers, of the horror they witnessed and the suffering of the officers and men on those carriers.

The *Zero* fighters attacked the dive bombers as they pulled out of their dives and harassed them until they flew well beyond the perimeters of the enemy task force. McClusky's plane was hit by a 20mm shell, and he was wounded by a shell splinter in a shoulder. Other planes were hit. Some of the pilots and gunners were wounded, but their planes were not shot down.

All the *Enterprise* planes were very low on fuel, and some had to ditch. The pilot and gunner of one plane were sighted in their life raft by an enemy destroyer and brought aboard to be interrogated. Under pressure, the pilot revealed the names of our carriers. A couple of days later, the pilot and his gunner had their hands and feet tied together, and then a weight was tied to them. They both were both dropped into the water and drowned. One other pilot and his gunner met a similar fate after being picked up by a different destroyer; however, they were first beaten to death and then tossed into the water. Four other *Enterprise* dive bombers ditched and were never found.

A fourth carrier, the *Hiryu,* was separated from the other carriers and partially hidden under a cloud layer. Attack aircraft from the *Hiryu* found the *Yorktown* and fatally damaged her with bombs and torpedoes, and her crew had to abandoned ship. Late that evening, an enemy submarine sighted the *Yorktown* with a destroyer, the *USS Hammann,* alongside. Working parties from the *Hammann* had been put aboard the *Yorktown* and had successfully repaired enough damage, where possible, so that it could be towed to Pearl Harbor. An enemy submarine sighted the *Yorktown* and fired a spread of torpedoes which hit both ships. As the *Hammann* was sinking, her depth charges were not on safe and exploded, sinking her with a large loss of lives. This doomed the *Yorktown,* and she finally sank.

As bad as it was losing the *Yorktown,* it was a tremendous American victory, considering the fact we had faced seemingly insurmountable odds against our forces winning the Battle of Midway. The Battle of Midway turned the tide of the war in less than ten minutes. The battle could just as easily have been a catastrophe for us if we had lost our three carriers.

Earlier that morning, just after I had landed on the *Hornet,* I was alone in our ready room. The *Yorktown* was being attacked by enemy dive bombers. Then there came the order, "Stand by to repel dive-bombing attack." This was the scariest moment I had ever experienced. Our ready room was right under the ship's island structure and protruded out under the flight deck. There are no fox holes on a ship. I wrapped a towel around my head, put on my flight gloves and took a seat as far back in the ready room as I could, hoping the island structure would absorb some of the bomb blast if we were hit near the ready room. Fortunately the *Hornet* was never attacked, and the tension eased. The aerial combat activity over the *Yorktown* was visible from *the Hornet,* and LT Ellenberg came in our ready room with a pair of binoculars and asked me if I wanted to go out on the catwalk of the island and watch a dogfight over the *Yorktown.*

For some reason I decided to stay in the ready room. A little later, I heard a loud noise that sounded like machine guns firing outside the ready room. A few minutes later, one of our squadron crew members carrying a bloody pair of binoculars rushed into our ready room and said, "LT Ellenberg has just been killed!" I'm shocked. But moments later, lo and behold, Ellenberg walks into the ready room holding a compress against his forehead with blood streaming down his face and onto his shirt. His lacerations were caused by metal fragments from the island structure when it was hit by bullets fired from the 50-caliber guns from a fighter plane that had landed on the flight deck. The pilot had been shot in his foot. Because of the injury, he made a hard landing which caused one the plane's landing gear to collapse. The engaged tailhook jerked the plane around until its nose was pointing at the island structure. At the same time the plane's guns fired killing all the marines manning a 40-millimeter gun position just aft of the island. Also killed was a lieutenant, the son of an admiral.

USS Yorktown - Listing after attack by Hiryu dive-bombers and torpedo planes - U.S. Navy photo

The *Hiryu* was located in the late afternoon, and the *Enterprise* and *Hornet* launched *SBDs* to attack the carrier. The flight included *Yorktown SBDs*, which were recovered by the *Enterprise*, after bombs and torpedoes had hit the *Yorktown*. The *Hornet* delayed launching the flight because the *SBDs* that had returned from Midway Island needed to be refueled and re-armed.

There were no fighter escorts available to protect our two *SBD* dive-bomber flights. The *Hiryu* was protected by a combat air patrol of *Zeros* that attacked the *Enterprise SBDs* as they were rolling into their dives. The *Zero* pilots, realizing they had to take out the *SBDs* in order to save the *Hiryu,* aggressively pressed home their attack by firing 20-mm canons and shooting down four of our *SBDs* as they rolled into their dives.

The first pilot shot down was Ensign Weber who had scored a bomb hit on the *Akagi* during the morning attack. Next were Ensigns Butler and Wiseman whose planes crashed into the sea almost simultaneously. Ensign Merrill's *SBD* was hit by 20mm canon shells with shell fragments damaging his flight controls and wounding his gunner. He was barely able to land his severely damaged plane on the *Enterprise*; subsequently, his plane and another *SBD* were judged unsalvageable and pushed off the flight deck into the water.

SBD Number B-11 Hornet Flight Deck - U.S. Navy photo

After launching our flight of sixteen dive bombers, we were still climbing to reach 12,000 feet in altitude. We had already turned to our heading for the *Hiryu* when my gunner told me, "Four fighters are turning in toward us!" The fighters turned out to be friendly *Wildcat F4Fs* from the *Enterprise's* combat air patrol. My tail-end position in the flight formation was the most vulnerable position of all when being attacked by fighters. That was a scary moment. The *Hornet SBDs* arrived over the vicinity of the *Hiryu* about fifteen minutes after she had been hit. As we neared the *Hiryu*, flying just above a layer of scattered clouds, black puffs of smoke from large caliber AA shells appeared ahead of us at our altitude. This was going to be my first time under fire. As we approached closer to the *Hiryu*, we could see that she was dead in the water and burning. Part of her forward flight deck had been blown up against the ships bridge. The only aircraft I observed was a lone cruiser's scout plane flying near the *Hiryu*. Where were the *Zeros?* They evidently didn't expect another attack and had descended down to sea level where they would be forced to ditch their planes as they ran out of fuel. This was a crowning moment in the battle. We now had complete control of the air. Our flight leader, seeing the *Hiryu* was fatally damaged, led us to a position to attack the heavy cruiser, the *Tone.*

Doomed Hiryu - massive damage to forward flight deck
U.S. Navy photo

The *Tone's* guns were putting up concentrated AA as our leading *SBD* entered its dive. After rolling into my dive and descending, I observed a huge bomb explosion dead center on the ship. As I continued diving, there were numerous smaller explosions in the water, missing about fifty yards to the port side of the cruiser.

My plane was accelerating too fast, possibly my dive brakes had not fully opened. As I approached my bomb release point and pressed the electrical switch to release the bomb, I knew it hadn't dropped. When the bomb is released, a "wishbone device" swings the bomb clear of the propeller, and you can feel the "wishbone" hit a stop. My bomb was hung up. Because of my abnormal speed, I frantically pulled back hard on my control stick to bring the nose up to break the dive. In doing so, I momentarily blacked out, but not before I was able to close the dive brakes. As the dive brakes close, your plane radically increases its speed. After regaining my full vision, I checked my airspeed indicator, and it was "pegged" at its maximum position. I had dived through a thin layer of clouds that obscured a destroyer, and I flew right over its fantail at about 300 feet. Every gun on the ship was firing at me, and shrapnel fragments were splashing like huge rain drops in the water below the plane. The planes tremendous acceleration made the Japanese gunners underestimate its speed. My airspeed indicator stayed pegged at its maximum reading. I thought the indicator was stuck, but it slowly returned to register a normal cruising speed of 145 knots. That tough old *SBD* had given me a wild ride. After getting clear of the destroyer, I was able to shake my bomb loose by manually releasing it.

Flying back to the *Hornet,* we flew over numerous yellow life rafts dotting the water. You felt sorry for those unfortunate pilots and crewmen down there. Then I wondered how many would be rescued. A torpedo pilot from the *Yorktown* was down there, and he survived 19 days before he was rescued. We flew over the stricken *Yorktown,* and she looked very forlorn in the gathering dusk.

After our flight landed on the *Hornet,* the pilots had gathered in the ready room. I asked the other pilots, "Where did those bombs come from that exploded near the port side the cruiser?" Somebody said, "Fisher didn't you see those *B-17's* above us. They almost dropped their bombs through our formation." If I had been a bombardier on one of those *B-17s* and after releasing my bombs and observing an explosion on that cruiser, I would have been convinced I had hit that ship.

The 12 June 1942 issue of the *New York Times* described how the *B-17s* had sunk all the Japanese carriers and won the Battle of Midway. Not so. Japanese postwar information confirmed the American dive bombers were the only aircraft to hit the enemy carriers. All our torpedo squadrons suffered terrible losses without one torpedo scoring a hit. Of the 45 torpedo planes launched from the *Hornet, Enterprise* and *Yorktown*, 43 were shot down, and the commanding officers of all three torpedo squadrons were killed. The sacrifices of the torpedo bombers set the stage for the *Enterprise* and *Yorktown* dive bombers to enter their dives unopposed by the *Zero* fighters. A huge tactical error had been made by the Japanese bringing their fighters down from high altitude for the massacre of the torpedo squadrons.

CHAPTER 11
THE BATTLE OF MIDWAY
5 JUNE 1942

The Saga of the Tanikaze

Our task force had retired to the east the night of 4 June to prevent engaging a superior Japanese surface force at night. The task force moved west again the next morning then launched a few *SBDs* to scout ahead of the task force. A contact report of a small Japanese task force consisting of two cruisers and some destroyers was received late in the afternoon. A flight of eighteen *Hornet* dive bombers was launched along with dive bombers from the *Yorktown* which had landed on the *Hornet* the day before. The *Enterprise* launched about twenty dive bombers. All the dive bombers would be carrying the smaller 500-pound bombs because we'd be flying almost to the limit of our combat range. Although sunset would be close to 2000, we would most likely end up making night carrier landings. Up to that time, most of us had only made one night landing during the *Hornet's* shakedown cruise in January, 1942. In tandem with our mission, the task force would be closing as much distance as possible to the target area.

At about 275 miles, we flew over a huge oil slick from the *Hiryu* that had finally been sunk early that morning by Japanese destroyers. We were too high to see any survivors that may have been in the water near the oil slick. I was hoping the CHAG, our flight leader, would abort the mission, but he continued on course until we sighted a single Japanese ship. It was first identified as a light cruiser, but later identified as the destroyer *Tanikaze.* The dive bombers ahead of us started to dive, and the *Tanikaze* increased its speed and employed evasive maneuvering. I expected to see some direct hits that would eventually sink the ship, but it was only bracketed by near misses. In my mind that ship was doomed, and a lot of men were going too die.

The *Tanikaze* was moving at maximum speed of over 30 knots and making quick, small circular changes in course instead of a tight circle like most of their ships did under attack. As I was getting in position to dive, two AA flak bursts behind me rocked the plane. I quickly rolled into a 70-degree dive. Immediately, I was faced with the destroyer's guns' staccato flashes and could see bombs exploding ahead of me making large circular patterns in the water. After I changed my aim twice, I missed close astern. I had underestimated the ship's speed. After recovering from the dive, I circled around behind the stern of the ship to take up a heading for the *Hornet.* And in doing so, I watched a *SBD* dive into the water and explode. It was LT Sam Adams, a *Yorktown* pilot. That day we lost a fine experienced pilot without one direct hit to the *Tanikaze.* In the afternoon of 4 June, Adams had led a search mission that located the fourth carrier, the *Hiryu.*

As the pilots completed their bombing runs, they immediately headed for the *Hornet* and *Enterprise.* None of us wanted to waste fuel or time trying to circle and get in formation. Instead, we formed a long line for the dreary flight back to the carrier. As we came within range of the carriers' radio homing device, my radioman told me he was receiving a very weak signal from the *Hornet* and a strong one from the Enterprise. The *Enterprise* was transmitting a different sector-code letter than the *Hornet.* We'd been briefed that both carriers would transmit the same code letters for each 20-degree sector radiating from each ship. These code letters indicated which sector you were in and the course to take. I elected to use the *Hornet's* code letter and was the first aircraft to land on the *Hornet* just as the small flush deck lights were turned on. By the time I got out of the cockpit, it was dark. The *Hornet* pilots that couldn't hear their ship's weak signal erroneously used the stronger signal from the *Enterprise,* and they became lost in the darkness.

The *Hornet's* powerful searchlight was turned on and pointed to a vertical position as a homing beacon for the lost pilots. The pilots who were able to see the light beacon found the carriers. One *Hornet* pilot reading almost empty on his last fuel tank decided to ditch while he still had engine power. As he was preparing to ditch into the water, his gunner yelled, "I see a light." The planned ditching was aborted, and the pilot made a straight-in approach to the *Hornet.* Just as the plane touched down on the flight deck and its tailhook engaged the wire, the engine quit. Two other *Hornet* pilots ran out of fuel in the landing pattern and had to ditch, and a destroyer rescued both of them and their crew members. A couple of *Hornet* pilots landed on the *Enterprise* and didn't know they were on the *Enterprise* until they tried to find their way to the ready room. The *Hornet* and *Enterprise* were of the same ship class, but each was configured a little differently.

The *Tanikaze* had over ninety bombs dropped on her including some from *B-17's* and she never suffered a direct hit. At the time, I thought someone on the ship's bridge was watching our individual dives as we approached our bomb release points and communicating his recommendations for quick course changes. I was right. There was a signalman, whose battle station was on the bridge, that had volunteered to be a lookout. He had laid on his back with his body partially protruding though a window hatch on the bridge. This way, he could see and track each dive bomber in its dive. He then passed his recommended course changes through a sound-powered telephone to the commanding officer who had taken over the helm. His actions saved the ship and its crew. His name was Masashi Shibata.

In 1991, two other squadron pilots and I met this *Tanikaze* crew member at the Hotel del Coronado in Coronado, California. We met in the hotel's patio garden. He was wearing his white Japanese naval uniform, carrying a bugle and a Japanese flag. I pinned a pair of gold aviator wings on his uniform and declared him an honorary naval aviator. Later that evening, the three of us and our wives joined Masashi Shibata and his wife for dinner in the hotel's famous *Crown Room.* During dinner, we swapped war stories, keeping our interpreter very busy. Mr. Shibata presented each of us with a small scale model of the *Tanikaze*. As we finished dinner, I proposed this toast to him and the crew of the *Tanikaze,* "We all know how the war ended. I want to propose a toast to a very brave man, Masashi Shibata. On that terrible day because of your heroic actions and the skilled seamanship of the ship's captain, the *Tanikaze* won her battle." It was an emotional moment for all, and Shibata broke down with tears rolling down his face. He quickly regained his composure and warmly thanked us all for our friendly reception.

The *Tanikaze* also participated in the carrier battle of Santa Cruz Island, 26 October, 1942. Later, the *Tanikaze* was sunk in the South Pacific, Shibata was severely wounded and his commanding officer was killed. He later became a successful and wealthy businessman in Japan and contributed to war memorials for both American and Japanese in the western Pacific areas. He has since died of cancer.

From left to right: CDR Don Adams, Mr. Masashi Shibata, CDR Clayton Fisher, and CAPT Roy Gee - Hotel del Coronado, 1991

The following is Shibata's personal narrative of the hell the Tanikaze's crew endured on that fateful afternoon 5 June 1941.

The Destroyer Tanikaze Returns from "The Sea of Death"
By Masashi Shibata

I was only 16 years of age when I volunteered for Japanese Naval Service on June 1, 1938. I studied as a signalman at Kure and studied seamanship at the naval school at Yokosuka. In May of 1942, I was assigned to the destroyer, Tanikaze.

Aboard the Tanikaze my duties included: standing watches, keeping the ships log, acting as a signalman for semaphore flags and light signals, as well as bugler. I also made astronomical observations, kept the ship's protocol and made ship wide announcements to the crew to relay the Captain's commands. My battle station was on the starboard side of the bridge at the 12-centimeter telescope.

The Tanikaze was commissioned in April of 1941 and was integrated into the 17th Destroyer Group.

The Tanikaze was a small ship with a total displacement of 2000 tons. Her maximum speed was 36 knots. She carried a crew of 239 men including the Captain.

The Tanikaze's crew was very close, almost like a family. We were completely united with Commander Katsumi, Captain of the Tanikaze. The intimate atmosphere was entirely different than that of a large battleship.

We were part of the First Task Force organized under Admiral Nagumo. The Tanikaze departed Hiroshima with the First Task Force on May 27, 1942.

The First Task Force was composed of the aircraft carriers: Akagi, Kaga, Hiryu and Soryu, two battle ships, two heavy cruisers and one light cruiser. There were also 12 destroyers in three groups. The Tanikaze was the command ship for the 17th destroyer group of four destroyers.

Search for the missing aircraft carrier Hiryu by the solitary Tanikaze.

Around noon on the 5th of June, the second day of the Battle of Midway, our forces had lost most of their aircraft, so we joined the Main Force under Admiral Yamamoto, Commander in Chief of the Fleet.

For the time being we thought we were safe. We received a semaphore message from the battleship Yamato ordering the Tamikaze to return to the Hiryu and rescue any survivors and sink the Hiryu if still afloat. Only the Tanikaze was on this mission which was considered suicidal.

We were unable to locate the Hiryu. The Captain of the Tanikaze decided the Hiryu had already sunk, so we changed course to join the Main Force.

Suddenly a watchman shouted, "enemy aircraft 130 degrees." I quickly took my binoculars and saw about 30 aircraft. The General Quarters alarm was sounded for the crew to take their anti-aircraft battle stations. Our ship's Captain addressed the crew over the ship's PA system and said, "We have fought well up to now, but this time we should be prepared to die with dignity."

Anti Aircraft Battle Stations

A starboard watchman shouted, "Many dive bombers approaching from aft starboard." Our Captain ordered, "Port helm, maximum full speed!"

The Captain ordered, "Open fire," and all the guns on the Tanikaze roared. One by one, more than 30 dive bombers attacked the Tanikaze dropping their bombs. Huge columns of water, higher then the masthead, surrounded the Tanikaze although no bombs hit the Tanikaze directly.

We needed somebody to watch the bombers and tell the Captain when to change and make evasive turns. I volunteered to be a lookout. I climbed out of a window hatch of the bridge and leaned my body back so I could see the sky and prepare for the next wave of dive bombers.

As each dive bomber approached, I shouted, "enemy bomber right, or bomber left." Captain Katsumi stood in front of the compass and gave commands to turn each time I shouted aircraft positions.

From my elevated position above the bridge I could see the pilots in their cockpits as some pulled out quite low. I can recall that some had goggles and white scarves. I was struck by the appearance of those American pilots' red faces, but I could see the fighting spirit of the Yankees.

No sooner had we again felt safe after the dive bombers had gone than the B-17s from Midway began to attack us in two waves. Thanks again to the superb ship handling of our Captain, we survived again.

We were attacked again by dive bombers from the Hornet. I had no time to count the aircraft, but it seemed to be more than 30.

Only Near Misses

One of the bombs, which damaged the stern near the water line and the aft starboard side of the hull, began to leak and had to be patched. Some bomb fragments had penetrated the # 2 gun turret and struck the magazine. All 6 gunners in the turret were burned to death. The gunnery crew of turret #3 hit a dive bomber, and it fell into the sea.

We fired almost all of our ammunitions, and the guns were so hot from heavy firing, that they were unable to fire. Later all the crew helped with removing 90-pound shells from the damaged turret. Our faces were blackened by the gun smoke, and our hands and clothes were soaked with sweat and covered with smoke dust.

The sun was going down. I never felt the sun could be such a blessing. Our Captain offered us cider and dry bread. I will never forget how tasty that bread was.

We worked all night to repair the damage and care for the wounded. In the morning at 6 a.m., we buried the bodies of the six dead seamen at sea. I played the bugle as a tribute to their memories. I could not stop my tears.

I felt the Tanikaze's remarkable survival in her evading 137 bombs from 75 bombs from 75 aircraft is a historical naval event. The Tanikaze was extremely lucky.

I felt fortunate to be one of the crew of this honorable ship, Tanikaze, and to assist Captain Katsumi at his side on the bridge."

Why could so many bombs miss the *Tanikaze?* Of course, a moving target like the narrow *Tanikaze* moving at over 34 knots and taking erratic, evasive course changes coupled with our pilot's lack of experience in dive bombing on fast-moving targets made it an extremely difficult target to hit. One good direct hit with a 500-pound bomb could have sunk the *Tanikaze.*

CHAPTER 12
THE BATTLE OF MIDWAY
6 JUNE 1942

Morning of 6 June

We now commenced what I considered the "mopping up" phase of the Midway Battle. The *Hornet* launched sixteen dive bombers to attack two cruisers and some destroyers. LCDR Widhelm, the executive officer of our scouting squadron, was our flight leader. He told us in our briefing, "I'm going to drive my bomb right down the smoke stack of the biggest cruiser we find." As we approached the big cruiser *Mikuma*, Widhelm pulled out of our formation, solo dived on the cruiser, and hit it squarely just behind the smoke stack. That was a great example of leadership. Now, all the rest of the pilots were hyped up wanting to get direct solid hits. On that mission, we lost a Scouting Squadron Eight pilot, probably shot down by AA fire. Nobody witnessed him get hit. He had told another squadron pilot he had a premonition he was going to get killed on that flight. He would be the only *Hornet* dive bomber killed during the battle.

Afternoon 6 June

The *Hornet* and *Enterprise* launched twenty dive bombers to finish off the *Mikuma* that had been bombed that morning. We found the cruiser smoking and dead in the water. There must have been over 200 survivors bobbing in the water, and they were being picked up by destroyers that were near the cruiser. Just ahead of us, our scouting squadron's flight hit the *Mikuma* with two 1,000-pound bombs, triggering a huge explosion with debris reaching over a thousand feet.

SBD dive bombers over Mikuma - U.S. Navy photo

Bomb devastation to Mikuma - U.S. Navy photo

As the destroyer pulled away from the vicinity of the cruiser, our squadron commander diverted our attack to bomb the destroyers. I selected a destroyer that was in a shallow turn and increasing its speed. The ship was not putting up any AA, probably because of the survivors exposed on the open deck. It was easy to line up for a glide-bombing run and I dropped my bomb from about 1,500 feet and my gunner told me we got a direct hit near the stern. The destroyer went dead in the water and settled at its stern. My commanding officer confirmed the hit. I learned later from post war Japanese accounts that the destroyer was the *Arsasho* and my bomb had killed thirty-nine men and there was terrible suffering among the wounded survivors. Due to the crew's superb damage control efforts, the ship managed to reach Wake Island.

The battle was over. All four of the enemy aircraft carriers had been bombed and sunk. A notable victory, since those four carriers were part of a six-carrier taskforce that had attacked Pearl Harbor on 7 December 1941.

After having flown all five of the attack missions launched from the *Hornet* and logging seventeen combat hours, I was emotionally drained and physically tired. It was difficult sitting in the officer's wardroom remembering the camaraderie and competitive joking between squadrons. Each squadron had its own table and now the torpedo and fighter squadron tables were empty. In the torpedo squadron's ready room, the pilot's caps and uniforms still hung on their hooks. As shipmates of the deceased pilots, we had the sad assignment of taking inventory of their personal effects, then packing them for shipment to their next of kin. It was a very emotional and depressing experience.

While the *Hornet* was en route to Pearl Harbor, the squadron pilots were not required to fly and we spent most of our time sitting around and sleeping in our ready room. A memorandum was passed around with the names of squadron pilots who were to receive the Distinguished Flying Cross. It took me a few seconds to realize my name wasn't on the list. It appeared I was the only pilot not getting a DFC. I was stunned and confused; I had flown all five of our squadron's combat dive bombing missions, some pilots had only flown three, and I had a confirmed direct hit on an enemy destroyer. After losing my cool, I stood up and let our squadron commander know, in no uncertain terms, how I felt. He told me, "Fisher, sit down and shut up," and then handed me a second memorandum. Only two names were on the memorandum; Ensign Gee and Ensign Fisher were being awarded the Navy Cross. Most naval aviators coveted the DFC and at first, I wasn't sure which one I would rather have, not knowing at the time the NC was the highest navy combat decoration. Anyway, I was embarrassed by my conduct and felt humble, especially when I found out each torpedo squadron pilot would receive a Navy Cross posthumously.

On 13 June, our squadron flew off the *Hornet* and landed on Ford Island, Pearl Harbor. The *Hornet* and *Enterprise* steamed by Diamond Head and finally docked at Pearl Harbor. This was closure for the Battle of Midway but there was another aircraft carrier battle looming in the *Hornet's* future.

CHAPTER 13
PEARL HARBOR AND SOUTH PACIFIC

Air Group Reorganization and Training

Our air group was assigned two new squadrons, Fighter Squadron One Seventy Two and Torpedo Squadron Six. On 19 June, the squadrons started intensive training. The dive-bomber squadrons practiced dive bombing on moving targets at sea, and the fighter tow planes pulled target sleeves over our flight formations for our rear gunners to shoot at. The gunners firing their twin 30-caliber guns usually severed the towline on the first run, which curtailed the practice for that day.

We practiced dive bombing in the mornings and had recreation in the afternoons. The evening curfew was strict. Servicemen had to be off the Honolulu streets by 1800. Believe it or not, while in Honolulu, we had to carry our gas masks at all times. Our squadron pilots usually spent the afternoons basking by the swimming pool; our skin was pale white from being on the *Hornet*. On one overcast day, I thought I didn't have to worry about getting sunburned. Because the sun's ultraviolet rays penetrated the overcast, I received the worst sunburn of my life. My shoulders were badly blistered and so sore I couldn't wear my parachute shoulder straps. There was a Navy directive that sunburns were no excuse for not carrying out your duties. So I flew for over a week with my parachute's shoulder straps unbuckled.

Some pilots would make bets on the number of hits they scored on the target boats. The lower you dropped your practice bombs, the easier it was to score. One pilot, who was getting the most hits, crashed into the sea and was lost. He just didn't pull out of his dive soon enough.

On 14 July, we flew off the Hornet to one of the Hawaiian Islands for target bombing practice, with live bombs, on a special range. We heard the Japanese had captured the island of Guadalcanal in the Solomon Islands, and we thought this was in preparation for retaking Guadalcanal. Little did we know that the Navy and Marines would have to recapture the island but at a great cost in ships, marines and aviators. Guadalcanal was retaken on 7 August. After a few days operating off the ship, the squadron flew back to Ford Island on 14 August and then back to the *Hornet* on 19 August. She was already on her course to the South Pacific for her last and final deployment. The *Hornet* would never again return to Pearl Harbor.

Deployment Again to the South Pacific

The *Hornet* deployed from Pearl Harbor with thirty Grumman *F4F* fighters with their wings removed, so more of them could be stowed on the hanger deck. These fighters would eventually be flown by Marine pilots, to Henderson Field on Guadalcanal.

On the first 200-mile search operations after leaving Pearl Harbor, our new commanding officer flew one of the 200-mile search sectors along with a wingman. The wingman returned alone and reported that the "Skipper's" plane had developed a fire in the cockpit, and he and his radioman had to bail out. Because the *SBD*'s two-man life raft was stowed in a compartment just behind the rear cockpit, they lost their life raft. Unfortunately, we didn't have the new type of parachute packs which included a single-man, rubber life raft until 1943. Three *SBDs* were launched with two-man life rafts loaded in the rear cockpits with the radiomen. The search area was huge, and the chances were slim they'd be found. If the two men were sighted, the rafts would be dropped as close as possible to them. Sad to say, the search was unsuccessful and had to be abandoned. Later on, pilots' life jackets were equipped with green-dye marker packets. These valuable markers, if they had had them, might have saved their lives. I've often wondered how long it took for those two men to die. Did they drown, or were they attacked by sharks?

As the *Hornet* was proceeding to the Coral Sea and Solomon Island area, the *Enterprise* was operating in the Coral Sea area helping to defend Guadalcanal from Japanese land-based bombers and carrier-based aircraft. The *Enterprise* had suffered considerable bomb damage from enemy dive bombers on 24 August and had to return to Pearl Harbor for major repairs. She would not arrive back in the Solomon's until 23 October. The *Hornet* task force continued to the South Pacific and began operating in the Coral Sea to the south of and near Guadalcanal. The *USS Saratoga* would join our task force on 30 August. I remember being happy that the *Saratoga* would be the duty carrier the next day because the *Hornet* pilots would have a day off from flying the lonely, daily 200-mile search missions.

The next morning, I was expecting to have a leisurely day, and I was in my room shaving when general quarters was sounded. It was announced that the *Saratoga* had just been hit by a torpedo. I ran from my room and continued running along a flight deck catwalk to get to our ready room, and while on the catwalk, I could see a huge column of smoke rising from the Saratoga. The electrical controls for the ships propulsion system had been damaged, and the *Saratoga* was dead in the water. Later a cruiser took her in tow to head for Noumea, New Caledonia. I had to fly an afternoon 200-mile search and could see black oil streaming behind the *Saratoga,* looking like a black highway. The propulsion system was repaired enough for the ship to make about ten knots. She finally arrived in Pearl Harbor 21 September.

One morning, it was announced that there would be a brief ceremony on the flight deck for awarding medals to pilots who had been cited during the Battle of Midway. Admiral Murray, our task force commander, whose flag flew on the *Hornet,* would make the presentations. The ceremony was scheduled for shortly before the afternoon's routine 200-mile searches would be launched. The recipients were lined up in formation in the hot sun opposite the ship's bridge. They announced each person's name and the decoration he was to receive. After the Admiral pinned the decoration on each recipient's uniform, he shook our hands and said, "Congratulations." The Admiral impressed me with his sincerity as he looked straight into my eyes and smiled. With my Navy Cross dangling from my uniform shirt, I had to rush down to our ready room and change into my flight suit as I was scheduled to fly the afternoon 200-mile search mission. As my plane was droning along on the search, I kept thinking about my Navy Cross. A strange feeling and apprehension that I might not make it back to the Hornet kept invading my thoughts. In the brief time in the ready room, I had barely glimpsed at the medal. Was I going to see it again?

The *Hornet* task force continued to operate in the Coral Sea south of Guadalcanal. Japanese submarines were active in the area, and the *Hornet* had luckily dodged two torpedoes fired by Japanese submarines. Everyday, we plotted a rectangular track of the task force on a map in our ready room, drawing overlapping lines from the track lines of the previous days. It was obvious the task force was vulnerable to a submarine attack. The *USS Wasp* had joined our task force, and she was the duty carrier on 15 September. Because of the break from flying, some of the *Hornet's* ship's officers and pilots, who were not on duty, were waiting to watch the movie *Dead End Kids* in the officers' wardroom. The movie had just started when we felt something like a thump, and then general quarters was sounded.

The aviation fuel tanks were located a few decks below the wardroom, and wasting no time, everybody scrambled for the nearest exits. Some of the officers jumped on the cloth covered tables and ran down their centers. Charging out of the wardroom, we met enlisted men hustling up a ladder from below the wardroom level. There was a traffic jam, so one officer yelled, "One officer, one man," bringing some semblance of order. After getting to our squadron ready room, messages were streaming across the teletype screen; the aircraft carrier the *Wasp*, the destroyer *O'Brian* and the battle ship *North Carolina* had been hit by torpedoes. I ran up on the flight deck and was shocked to see the Wasp was aflame with a huge cloud of smoke billowing up. She was dead in the water and listing to her starboard. The *O'Brian's* keel had been badly damaged, but with superior damage control, she didn't sink and finally made it back to Pearl Harbor. The *North Carolina* suffered minor damage and was picking up speed.

USS Wasp torpedoed by Japanese submarine - 15 September 1942 - U.S. Navy photo

USS O'Brien torpedoed - USS Wasp burns - U.S. Navy photo

All the damage had been done by the Japanese submarine *I-19* firing a spread of six torpedoes. Three torpedoes hit the *Wasp,* and the others passed beyond her. One hit the *O'Brian,* another the battleship *North Carolina,* and the last torpedo ran to fuel exhaustion. The *Wasp* had her starboard side ripped wide open, and with uncontrollable gasoline fires and exploding ammunition, the resulting fires doomed the ship. The explosion from the warhead of one torpedo obliterated the officers quarters, and a dozen pilots died, some in their bunks. The *Hornet* recovered some of the *Wasp's SBD* dive bombers that were airborne when the *Wasp* was torpedoed. All the *Wasp's* planes were new and very welcomed gifts by the *Hornet* pilots. The *Hornet* was now the only aircraft carrier left operating in the South Pacific.

On 26 September, the *Hornet* launched the *SBDs* to fly to an airfield at Noumea, so as to have the needed hanger deck space to assemble the wings on the fighters. *Hornet* fighter pilots flew the reassembled *F4F* fighters to Noumea airport. Later *SBDs* flew the Hornet fighter pilots, in their rear cockpits, back to the Hornet. The Noumea Airport was too congested with all our Navy planes, so our squadron was ordered on 7 October to fly our planes to the Island of Efate, which was part of the New Hebrides island group.

My personal log book shows I flew slightly over six hours to Efate and six hours on the return flight. LT Fred Bates led the flight navigating by dead reckoning. We had to fly on top of overcast for the last one hundred miles. The gas gauge on my last main tank was reading close to empty, and my eyes were glued to the gauge. LT Bates took us down through the overcast, and we had to hold very tight wing positions. We broke below the clouds right over Efate! If our estimated wind direction had changed while we were en route, we would have missed Efate because we didn't have enough fuel to search for the island. That was the longest flight I ever flew in a single-engine airplane. Fortunately, our parachute riggers had made special 8-inch-thick foam-rubber cushions that were placed on top of the thin standard seat cushions, so we didn't have paralyzed butts. I don't remember even having a canteen of water.

We stayed at Efate until 7 October and lived in metal Quonset huts.

Coconuts woke us at night hitting the roofs, and we could hear the rats scurrying around under the huts. A Marine fighter squadron was using the same field. They had some liquor with them; however, they didn't share their good stuff. Instead, they gave us two bottles of Crème de Menthe liqueur. They also had not provided any ice. The weather was humid, and without ice, nobody bothered to drink it. Of course, it might have made a good mouthwash.

A wily Frenchman, always decked out in white clothes and a straw hat, owned the small general store in the only village on the island. The store smelled of curry powder, which seemed to be his largest single inventory. We haggled over some bottles of wine that contained about an inch of sludge on the bottoms. Back at our Quonset huts, we were set to have a party. I took one slug and that was enough. It was vile stuff. Some of the more courageous drinkers got drunk and they paid for it. One pilot carried his cot outside the hut and passed out lying in the sun. We finally had to carry him back into the hut. When he sobered up the next morning, he told us, "I thought I heard bells ringing and was on a streetcar back in Philadelphia." Others lost their lunches accompanied by horrendous hangovers.

There was another small, almost barren, island next to Efate, and for a dollar, a native would take you out to the island in an outrigger canoe. As I walked by one native hut, I saw canned food stacked up and a portable Singer sewing machine. As a sequel to visiting the little island and much later, I had the opportunity to talk to the famous author James A. Michener, who wrote about the beautiful tropical island of Bali Hai in his book, *"South Pacific."* I met him when he was aboard the *USS Essex* during the Korean War. Finally I became bold enough to ask him if he had based his story on this island. He laughed and told me that it was, indeed.

On 7 October, we were ordered to fly back to the *Hornet* at Noumea. When we were all taxiing out to the runway, some Marine fighters followed our planes. We knew they were going to "buzz" us and make simulated gunnery runs on our formation as we left. The taxiways and the runways were covered with white coral, crushed rock. When you pulled full-engine power to take off, huge clouds of white dust were stirred up. KB White and I were flying the last two planes, and we decided to sit at the head of the runway, hold our positions with our brakes and pull full power on our engines for a few minutes. In doing so, we created huge clouds of dust which delayed the Marine fighter pilots from taking off close behind us. Our tactic worked. After we were airborne, we stayed low over the water until we were a few miles at sea. They never caught up to our formation. We had spoiled their fun.

CHAPTER 14
BATTLE OF SANTA CRUZ
26 OCTOBER 1942

Prelude

Before 23 October, the *Hornet* was the only carrier operating in the South Pacific. The *Enterprise* and *Hornet* task groups joined forces and moved to the northwest to interpose between the Guadalcanal and a Japanese carrier task force operating between Truk and Guadalcanal. This task force of carriers, *Shokaku*, *Zuikaku*, *Zuiho*, and *Junyo*, eight heavy cruisers, two light cruisers and twenty-eight destroyers was the strongest naval force since the Battle of Midway.

The Japanese army had been slowly reinforcing their troops on Guadalcanal. They had set the date of 22 October for their army to retake the airfield on Guadalcanal in order to use it for operations and an airstrip for their carrier planes. Our Marines upset the enemy plans by driving back infantry attacks on the airfield.

The Japanese carrier task forces had veered southeast, and the *Hornet* and *Enterprise* were now approaching head-on toward the enemy forces. The stage was now set for the carrier battle which would later be named the Battle of the Santa Cruz Island. This is an account of the *Hornet* dive bombers during the battle.

The Battle

During the late afternoon of 25 October, I was watching a card game in our fighter squadron's ready room. There were the usual information messages about the *Hornet's* course, speed and wind velocity flowing across the lighted teletype screen in the front of the ready room. Suddenly, a new message came across the screen. Enemy contact — carrier task force — position 350 miles NW. We're close to "strike" distance! This got the pilots' attention, and the card game came to an abrupt end. I hurried back to my squadron's ready room. Our pilots were already bent over their navigation flight boards plotting in our task force's position and the enemy's. Early that night, the *Hornet's* crew went to their battle stations, and the pilots to our ready rooms. We remained in our ready rooms the entire night.

Around midnight, I remember taking a short break from our ready room with a small group of dive-bomber pilots. We stood on the flight deck next to the island structure looking at the bright moon illuminating the night. It was almost like daylight. We all had the same thought, there was enough light to dive-bomb those carriers, and surprise them like we did at Midway.

Hornet's Initial Launch of Sixteen SBD Dive-bombers

All the pilots expected the *Hornet's* aircraft would be launched at dawn, but nothing happened. The task force commander was waiting for more accurate Japanese position reports. All I could think about was an enemy early surprise attack and having bombs come crashing down on out planes on the flight deck. Finally, we were given the command, "Pilots, man your planes." I was assigned to fly the left wing position on LT Bates. This pleased me because he was the best and most experienced pilot in our squadron. The initial flight launched was sixteen dive-bombers; eight Scouting Squadron's *SBDs* and eight Bombing Squadron's *SBDs*. LCDR Widhelm, now the commanding officer of the Scouting Squadron would lead the flight.

Over the bullhorn boomed the command, "Start all engines." While taxiing forward to the takeoff spot, flight-deck crew members held up chalkboards with a great morale-builder message which relayed that there was one more enemy aircraft carrier. We had been briefed before we left our ready room that we would have only four *F4F*

Wildcat fighters from our fighter squadron to escort the dive bombers. Were we on a suicide mission? I was too busy checking out my engine and getting my plane ready for takeoff to think too much about what would lie ahead.

Flight deck personnel holding caulk boards - telling pilots there was one more Japanese carrier - U.S. Navy photo

I taxied my plane to the take-off spot, revved up my engine to full power, lowered my landing flaps and rolled down the flight deck. As I cleared the flight deck ramp, my plane settled toward the water due to the weight of my 1,000-pound bomb. That little drop gave the plane a couple more knots of speed. After retracting my wheels, I could hold my altitude as the plane slowly started climbing. As I reached 200 feet, I slowly eased my landing flaps up in increments. I had expected to fly upwind and then start a 180-degree turn inside of LT

Bates because he would be coming downwind to join up on the formation. However, Bates was already passing me going downwind and climbing. Quickly adding full throttle, then doing a hard left turn, I started climbing to close up on the formation. After joining the formation and taking my wing position, I was finally able to reduce my engine from full power. Now, I was very concerned about how much extra fuel I had consumed trying to join the formation. You burned a lot at full throttle.

Red Meat Balls, Lots of Them

About thirty minutes later, the formation had reached nearly 10,000 feet. LT Bates got my attention by repeatedly pointing upward. What was he pointing at? Up there was a tight formation of silver enemy aircraft glistening in the sun against a clear blue sky! All those planes had big, bright-red, solid circles called "meatballs." Evidently their flight leader didn't see us, so their *Zero* fighters stayed in formation. A little later their fighters sighted and surprised the pilots of our torpedo planes, which were flying well behind and below our dive - bombers, and shot two of them down. About forty-five minuets later, we passed over a small Japanese task force of two cruisers, the *Tone* and *Chikuma.* They were escorted by destroyers; one was the *Tanikaze,* which had been in the Midway battle. There were seven *Zero* fighters protecting the task force. This small task force could have been a decoy ahead of the enemy carrier task force. We continued on course; our primary objective was the enemy carriers.

The *Zero* fighters engaged our four fighters and quickly shot down two of them. The other two fighters, trying to survive, disappeared into some clouds. That was the end of our fighter support. We were on our own. I heard my gunner shooting his guns in short bursts. We were now going to be under intermittent and, ultimately, under continuous attack by the *Zeros.* I was startled when I caught a glimpse of what I first thought was a pilot's body spinning down and passing close to the right side of our formation. It was a *Zero* fighter's gasoline belly tank jettisoned from a *Zero* flying above our formation. I heard my gunner firing again. The *Zeros* were trying to attack us from above and to our rear. A *Zero* that had just made a steep dive on our formation pulled out too hard, which, in turn, caused it to shed its wings and then sent it spiraling into the sea. We flew through some clouds and shook the fighters for a short time, but they attacked again when we cleared the clouds.

A Zero made a diving attack trying to ram Widhelm's plane head on to takeout our leader. Widhelm fired his two 50-caliber guns that were synchronized to fire through his propeller into the engine of the Zero exploding its engine. Widhelm ducked his plane down and missed the flying debris of the burning Zero. I watched another Zero with two red bands on its fuselage attempt to make a high-side gunnery run on Widhelm's plane and then abort the run. KB White, said, "It looked like he was stalking us." The *Zero* made a second attempt to hit Widhelm's plane. This time, the pilot made a successful high-side — almost full-deflection — gunnery run. I watched two long, yellow-blue flashes spit from the *Zero*'s 20mm guns. Widhelm's engine was hit and the engine started streaming black oil smoke through our formation. His engine finally seized, and he dropped out of the formation and successfully ditched. He and his gunner were later rescued by a *PBY*. Ironically, the *PBY*'s pilot was a former flight student of Widhelm's who had trained at Pensacola.

LCDR Vose, our squadron commander, took over as our leader. The *Zero* attacks increased in intensity. KB White had a badly damaged aileron, and he was hit in his left hand. He couldn't keep his position and dropped out of formation but was able to land later on the *Enterprise*. LTJG Grant's plane was hit. His gunner was either badly wounded or killed, and an ammo-belt was seen hanging out of his cockpit flapping in the slipstream against the side of the plane. LTJG Carter, also flying in our rear-position "diamond" section, was having problems staying in formation during the leadership change. Carter's plane was forced completely out of the formation, but he regained his position by diving under the formation and then sharply pulling back up into the formation. He observed Grant's plane drop out of our formation and watched *Zeros* shooting at his plane as it was going down. Carter's plane's had a propeller blade hit, a hole knocked in it, which unbalanced the propeller causing his engine to shake and vibrate. In the last few miles, Vose kept turning the formation in slow shallow evasive turns. Flying in the tail end of the formation was like being on the end of a mild "crack the whip," and I was getting sucked out of position. The only way I could get back in formation was to dive back underneath the formation and pull up to regain my wing position. The 1,000-pound bomb made the plane sluggish to maneuver. A long burst of 7.7mm bullets hit my plane, severed a hydraulic line and hydraulic fluid started running down into the bilges below my feet.

As we were approaching the carrier task force, I caught a glimpse of a cruiser on the perimeter of the task force and then, through some broken clouds, spotted a carrier, the *Shokaku*. As our formation was approaching the position to commence our dives, I checked my hydraulically operated dive brakes. The brakes wouldn't open. As the planes ahead of me opened their dive brakes and began rolling into their dives, all I could do was follow the last plane down in a "clean dive." But, I had to move away from their dive paths so that I wouldn't overrun them. The dive bombers with their dive brakes extended would reach close to a maximum dive speed of about 240 knots. My plane accelerated rapidly to over 300 knots. Because of my excessive high speed, I started pulling out above 2,000 feet and then continued down until I leveled out low over the water. My dive path had taken me well ahead of the *Shokaku*.

While Carter was diving on the *Shokaku* and just as he was pulling out of his dive, his gunner was wounded when a shell from the *Shokaku* exploded below his cockpit position. Shrapnel lacerated his gunner's feet, and a piece lodged in his leg. He managed to stop the bleeding later with supplies from a first-aid kit. Carter was able to make it back to the *Enterprise*. He had to fight his way through a swarm of other planes trying to get into the landing pattern but was waved off by the LSO. He ignored the wave off, continued his approach and landed successfully. Vose and Bates got direct hits with their 1,000-pound bombs on the *Shokaku*. We made our dives with the cockpit hatch open, and a small splintered piece of the *Shokaku's* flight deck was later found in Bate's cockpit. He had flown through flying debris from a bomb blast of the plane ahead of him. After his dive, LTJG Gee from our squadron was able to join up with two of Scouting Eight's squadron aircraft piloted by LT Moore and LTJG

Kirkpatrick. A *Zero* attacked them, and a 7.7mm slug grazed Moore's neck. His gunner was hit in the arm. Kirkpatrick's gunner was also wounded. The *Zero* ran out of ammunition, and the pilot then flew along side the dive-bomber formation, saluted the pilots and flew off. Was it a gesture of respect or mockery? When I finally leveled off at 300 feet, my gunner yelled, "We got a *Zero* on our tail!" Putting it mildly, it was a horrifying feeling. I couldn't out maneuver the *Zero*. With a *Zero* on its tail, a *SBD* dive bomber has a slight advantage over a single fighter because of the gunner's rapid-firing, twin 30-caliber guns. So I dove closer to the water where the fighter couldn't get in a position below us — a dangerous spot because the gunner couldn't position his guns to bear down on the *Zero*. My gunner, ARM 3/c Ferguson, practically shot off our rudder trying to hit the *Zero*. Both wings were riddled with small jagged holes after being hit with 7.7mm bullets. One bullet passed between my legs, shattering my engine's cylinder temperature gauge.

Finally, the *Zero* fired his 20mm cannons, and a shell exploded in the radio transmitter located behind my armored seat. A radio-frequency manual was blown to bits with confetti flying all over the cockpit. The concussion from the exploding shell inside the confines of the cockpit canopy felt like I had been hit a hard blow on top of my head. Simultaneously, I felt a red-hot burning sensation in my right arm just below my shoulder. Shrapnel fragments flying around in the cockpit had hit my upper right arm just above the elbow. Momentarily stunned, I had lost my vision, but my mind was visualizing the shimmering, wavering faces of my mother and Annie. I didn't want to die, but felt completely helpless. After recovering from the shock of the concussion and as my vision cleared, the *Zero* fighter, with its big red "meatball" insignia, was flying off my right wing, just like a wingman. The pilot was staring at me! When our eyes met, he drifted back behind us. Ferguson had been shot in both thighs with 7.7mm bullets and a piece of shrapnel had gouged some flesh out of the calf of his right leg. Ferguson managed to reload his jammed guns, in spite of his wounds, and waited for the *Zero* to get into firing range. The *Zero's* pilot evidently felt we were cold turkey and moved slowly into position for the kill. Ferguson fired first and hit the engine of the *Zero*. The *Zero*, with its engine smoking, pulled up sharply away from us and then disappeared. We had miraculously survived; Ferguson had not panicked. He had saved both our lives. After picking up my compass heading for the *Hornet* and checking my wrist watch, it read 1200. My arm throbbed with pain, and my flight glove kept filling up with blood which I emptied into the bilge below my feet. I used my left thumb to press into my right armpit hoping the pressure on the artery would reduce the bleeding. The blood was mixing with the hydraulic fluid in the bilge below my feet, and I became concerned about how much blood I could lose and still remain conscious. Ferguson assured me he was okay, in spite of being wounded, and he never complained. After flying for what seemed like thirty minutes, I checked my wrist watch, it was still 1200! My watch had stopped. I had forgotten to wind it. I'm on course for the *Hornet,* but haven't a clue how far we've flown. After flying for what seemed like a long time, I started looking for the *Hornet.* We had unlimited visibility, but I was still concerned about whether I should stay on our course. I could be far enough off course and miss the *Hornet.* I almost decided to turn south, and if we had to ditch, we might have a slim chance of floating toward one of the Solomon Islands. Mulling this over, I then spotted a *Zero* passing directly underneath us headed in the opposite direction, followed by two Japanese dive bombers. That was the only time I was relieved to see a *Zero.* Now I knew we were on the correct heading and could not be too far from the *Hornet.*

Douglas SBD Dive Bomber - U.S. Navy photo

The *Hornet* Dead in the Water

When the *Hornet* came into view, I was shocked. She was dead in the water and listing to her starboard side, and the flight deck was covered with yellow foam and debris. A destroyer hovered on her port side, and a cruiser was standing by. This would be my last view of the *Hornet*.

My last view of Hornet – U.S. Navy photo

A Japanese squadron's commander flying a dive bomber had deliberately crashed his plane into the *Hornet's* signal bridge above the island structure. The plane's engine and the unexploded bomb landed in our squadron's ready room. Fortunately, the bomb didn't explode and kill the three pilots who were in the ready room. Another bomb from a dive bomber penetrated the flight deck and exploded on the hanger deck. Unfortunately, many of our squadron's ordinance men and engine mechanics were huddled on their hands and knees with their heads down on the hanger deck where the bomb exploded near them, and there were a lot of casualties. It was a bloody mess. Unlike on land, there are no fox holes on a ship.

Japanese dive-bomber squadron commander crashing diving into Hornet - U.S. Navy photo

USS Hornet under attack by Japanese aircraft - U.S. Navy photo

I could see the *Enterprise* dimly in the distance east of the *Hornet*. As I closed the distance to the *Enterprise*, I saw a lot of aircraft swarming around in the landing flight pattern, and I knew I'd have to fight for a position to try and land. If any aircraft made a bad landing, the deck would have to be cleared before landings could continue. Also, I didn't have operable landing flaps and wouldn't be able to slow down enough to make a safe carrier landing. The fuel gauge for my last main fuel tank was pegging close to empty. Now my only chance was to ditch my plane in front of what I first thought was a destroyer. As I approached the ship, I stayed on a parallel course showing only my side profile. We were supposed to do a 360-degree recognition turn to indicate we were friendly aircraft, but I didn't want to waste what little fuel I had left to make the turn. Finally, I was positioned about a quarter mile ahead and to the starboard of the ship, which I now recognized as a cruiser, the *USS Juneau*. I never pointed the nose of my plane at the ship hoping to be recognized as a friendly aircraft rather than an enemy aircraft on the attack.

Ferguson jettisoned his guns as we prepared to ditch. Dive bombers didn't have shoulder straps like the fighters, so our squadron parachute riggers had improvised a single strap that crossed our chests. I tightened the chest strap and lowered my seat as far as possible, so I wouldn't gouge out an eye if my head hit the gun sight. The sea wasn't too rough, but I was worried about the swells. I decided to get as close to the water as possible, so I slowed the plane down. I gradually pulled the nose of the plane up and kept adding engine power to hold my altitude, which was a technique called "hanging it on the prop." I had hoped to ditch at the lowest possible airspeed because I didn't have landing flaps to slow the plane down. Also, I didn't want the plane to stall out, enter a spin, or dig a wing tip in the water and cartwheel. As the plane started to shake approaching a stall condition, I chopped the throttle. I don't remember hitting the water because I had been temporarily knocked unconscious when my forehead smacked into the instrument panel. The water rapidly filled the cockpit reviving me. Ferguson had already pulled the life raft out of the side of the aircraft, inflated it, and was pulling me up under my arms to help me out of the cockpit. We were able to climb into the raft from off the left wing before the plane sank. Fortunately, the life raft which was stowed just behind the rear cockpit hadn't been punctured by the many 7.7mm bullets that had hit the plane.

The *Juneau* came along side our raft, and sailors threw us lines. I was able to catch the first line and wrap it around my wrists, and Ferguson tackled my legs. The *Juneau* was moving slowly, and Ferguson and I were being dragged along with the raft. I almost had my shoulders dislocated when the line tightened. The *Juneau* had a large cargo-type net rigged down the side of the hull to assist in rescue operations. Sailors climbed down the net, looped a line under my arms and hauled me up on the main deck. Ferguson in spite of his wounds in both legs climbed unassisted up the net. We had been rescued in about four minutes according to the official Juneau's log.

Excerpts from ships log:

1201 – ENTERPRISE reports enemy planes bearing 240 degrees, 10 miles.

1207 – Smoke on water bearing 289 degrees. Appears to be shot down plane.

1210 – Heavy AA fire over T.F.16. bearing 090 degrees. Changed course to 085 degrees to intercept. (Note- Task force 16 included Enterprise)

1212 – Friendly SBD3 plane, No. B-8 of BomRon 8, landed in water 1000 yards on starboard bow.

1216 – Picked up crew of 2 men of above plane with ship. Men wounded and sent to sick bay.
1217 – Resumed course 085 degrees, speed 30 knots to join T.F. 16.

How lucky could I get that day! I felt like the cat with nine lives.

USS Juneau - Light AA cruiser- 16 twin 5-inch gun mounts – numerous 40mm guns - U.S. Navy photo

Aboard the Juneau

Ferguson and I were supported by sailors as we were led stumbling down to a small sick bay. CDR Neff, the ship's doctor, examined my arm. My elbow joint was exposed, and I had lost some flesh just above the elbow. The doctor asked me if I could move my thumb. I could move it and the doctor told me, "You're one lucky son of a bitch!" It was a flesh wound with no damage to the tendons or bone joint. If the shrapnel had hit an inch lower, my elbow joint would have been shattered. The doctor dusted the wound with sulfa powder, loosely bandaged the arm and put me in a bunk. He threw blankets over me and told me I was in severe shock and to stay in the bunk or I could die.

The ship's space Ferguson and I were in was one deck below the main deck and under a twin 5-inch gun turret. Shortly thereafter, the task force came under an aerial torpedo attack, and the *Juneau,* which was a new type AA light cruiser, let loose with all its 5-inch guns. The whole ship shook. Lying in the bunk, I wanted to see what was going on.

USS Enterprise under attack by Japanese aircraft - U.S. Navy photo

Finally, the firing stopped, and I realized I hadn't relieved myself for over six hours and needed to visit a head – a toilet. A young seaman with a broken leg in a cast shared the space. I asked him where the nearest head was, and he pointed at a ladder that was used to get up to the next deck. After climbing out of the bunk, wearing a white bathrobe, I started up the ladder. I became nauseous and a little disorientated, but I finally reached the deck. Breathing in the wonderful fresh air, I moved over to the handrail on the port side, just below the ship's bridge, and vomited over the side. Then the ship accelerated and began a hard turn to starboard making it tilt sharply to the port side. I quickly grabbed the handrail to stay on my feet. Looking around, I could see 40mm-gun crews with their steel helmets, flash clothing, goggles, gloves and life jackets. The men in the open had to be protected from muzzle blasts. Those gunners must have thought I looked like a ghost standing out there in the open. Doctor Neff, a big man, came down from his battle station on the bridge, grabbed me, threw me over his shoulder and hauled me back down to the bunk. He put the blankets over me and said, "God damm it, Fisher, now stay there!"

That night after the *Juneau's* crew came off their battle stations, Dr. Neff and his corpsmen put Ferguson and me "out" with sodium pentothal and cleaned our wounds. Ferguson and I had a bad night after the drug had worn off. By morning, my arm had hemorrhaged, and my bunk was a bloody mess.

Dr Neff visited me in the morning and asked, "What the hell possessed you to go up on deck?" I told him I had desperately needed to relieve myself and told him about the seaman's directions. Doctor Neff asked the seaman, "Why didn't you tell LT Fisher there was a head right behind his bunk?" The seaman said, "That's an enlisted man's head."

The first day I could eat in the officer's wardroom, I sat next to the ship's gunnery officer. He asked me, "Why didn't you make the 360-degree recognition turn when you approached the Juneau?" I told him, "The fuel gauge was starting to read empty on my last available gas tank." He told me, "I was just ready to give the order to fire our guns, when a sailor yelled *SBD!*" The *Juneau's* guns would have blasted my plane out of the air like a clay pigeon. I was lucky some *Juneau's* sailor had stayed awake in his aircraft recognition training class.

The *Juneau* had also picked up a fighter pilot and a torpedo plane crew. The fighter pilot from the *Enterprise* was Andy Loundes, who had been my roommate during flight training at NAS Jacksonville - the buddy I had walked off demerits for. It was a small world. We were now new short-term shipmates. Andy wrote a letter to Annie for me because of my incapacitated right arm. Previously Andy and I had met back in Pearl Harbor, and in a self-deprecating way, he said, "Fisher, all the good guys are getting killed in this war. You and I are going to survive it." Later, in a freak accident, Andy was killed. He was flying a fighter plane and was going to strafe a target being towed behind a ship. When he fired his guns, his plane blew to pieces in midair.

The task force headed into port at Noumea, New Caledonia. The entrance channel was heavily mined for submarine protection, and the ships proceeded in single file, zigzagging through an intricate approach path. We passed close to a destroyer, the *USS Smith DD 378,* that had its forward-gun turret blown apart. The turret was a burned out shell. A Japanese torpedo plane that had been hit by AA and was burning while trying to torpedo the Enterprise continued on and crashed with its torpedo intact between the two forward gun mounts of the *Smith.* The burning wreckage of the plane fell overboard and sank. The torpedo remained on the ship, and because of the fire's heat, the torpedo exploded. There were fifty-one fatalities.

After the *Juneau* dropped anchor in Noumea's harbor and before being transferred to the Navy hospital ship, *USS Solace*, I met with the *Juneau's* commanding officer, Captain Swenson, and asked why he risked his ship rescuing Ferguson and me. He grinned modestly and shrugged his shoulders. We both knew he shouldn't have risked his ship and 700 crew members to rescue us in the midst of a battle.

On 15 November, the *Juneau* was torpedoed and sunk. Captain Swenson and Dr. Neff were lost. Only ten men survived, and I wouldn't become aware of this terrible tragedy until I returned to California.

CHAPTER 15
USS SOLACE AND LURLINER

O n the 31 October, they transferred me from the *Juneau* to the Navy hospital ship, the *USS Solace,* which was anchored in the harbor at Noumea. The *Solace* medical staff was screening the casualties from the *Hornet* and other ships anchored in Noumea Bay. It was a sobering sight seeing the wounded men lying in gurneys on the main deck waiting to be tagged for disposition. The seriously injured were going to be sent to hospitals in Australia and New Zealand.

A Navy corpsman examined my medical record from the *Juneau* and gave me an identification marked with a red "A," meaning I was ambulatory. A nurse assigned me a space with two beds. A grotesque-looking patient was lying on layers of wax paper in one of the beds. The flesh on his head and hands looked like they were charred black, and he was swearing and carrying on about his predicament. I had qualms about sharing a room with him, until I discovered he was Duffy, the *Hornet's* Chief Electrician.

Solace to Lurliner

Later that day the *Lurliner*, a peacetime luxury liner, now a troop ship, was brought along side the *Solace*. A gangway was rigged between the two ships. That evening was Halloween, and resembling ghosts and goblins, the ambulatory patients in white bathrobes with black faces and hands that looked like black claws paraded across the gangway to the *Lurliner*. The non-ambulatory wounded were carried across on stretchers. Then some young marines, still on board the troop ship waiting to be deployed to Guadalcanal, were watching the transfer of the wounded. You wondered what was going through the minds of those young marines. At that time the Marines were fighting desperately to hold on to Guadalcanal. The next evening as dusk was approaching, the *Lurliner* slipped out of the harbor snaking through a marked path in the mined areas.

Our Navy treated most burn cases with tannic acid, which would cake where it was applied. Some of these men had been transferred to a New Zealand cruiser, and the medics treated burn cases with a black aniline dye. Their corpsmen walked around with flit guns loaded with the dye, and they sprayed the black dye over the caked tannic acid. It made the flesh look like it was charred black. In first and second-degree burns, the black crust would peel off and leave pink skin, so most of the men's burns were not as bad as they looked.

Honeymoon Suite

I liked telling my friends I spent eighteen days in the "honeymoon suite" on the *Lurline,* not with my bride, but with six other officers sharing the suite and sleeping in three-tier narrow bunks. Two of the men were from the *Hornet's* ships company: the Assistant Medical Officer, Dr. McAteer, and Chief Electrician Duffy. Dr. McAteer sustained chest injuries after being blown against a bulkhead. Duffy was enjoying a candy bar when he was burned from a bomb blast while standing under a ship's ventilator. The bomb blast sent a hot heat wave down the opening of a ventilator burning Duffy's head and face.

Duffy was a born storyteller, and he'd regale us with outrageous tales of his exploits. He had been everywhere, seen everything and done everything - a true sailor. These two Irishmen had lively senses of humor. Duffy would embellish his sea stories with the doctor egging him on. Their never-ending tales and humor eased our boredom on the eighteen-day trip back to San Diego.

The first day we entered the officer's dining room, Duffy's black head and hands got the attention of a pompous Army colonel. He objected strenuously to Duffy's appearance and told us Duffy had to leave the dining room.

The blackened, caked tannic acid on Duffy's head was starting to peal off. We decided if we could get Duffy in a bathtub and soak his head and hands, we could get him presentable enough to eat in the dining room. The *Lurliner* had rationed all fresh water and we were taking salt-water baths. We received permission from a ship's officer to fill a bathtub with fresh water, Duffy got into the tub and with soaked towels we gently rubbed Duffy's head. After successfully removing the caked tannic acid, we cracked up laughing. Little Duffy looked beautiful, like a pink baby. That evening we proudly escorted our baby into the dining room right past the pompous colonel's table. The *Lurliner* still had civilian waiters serving the officer tables and our waiter served us goodies like thick soups and molded ice cream deserts left over from the peacetime cruises. The pompous colonel demanded some of the same deserts, but our waiter politely told him only the wounded patients were being served these special treats. What sweet revenge.

The ballroom on the *Lurliner* was set up as a sick bay, to treat patients. While I was waiting to have my arm examined, I was watching a doctor remove the burned skin from the back of the hand of a non-flying officer from our squadron. LT Cartwright, our squadron administrative officer, had been there when the Japanese dive-bomber's plane had crashed into the signal bridge, and the bomb and engine came through the flight deck into our ready room. Although the bomb did not detonate, Cartwright and LTJG Swope from Scouting Squadron Eight received burns from flaming gasoline. Cartwright was in so much pain while the doctor was trying to clean the burned area on the back of his hand that he fainted.

The doctor told me he needed to remove the proud-flesh that had formed over my arm wound, or I would end up with an ugly scar. He applied silver nitrate on the area and wrapped a loose bandage around my arm. He also told me it would be very painful for about an hour while the silver nitrate slowly burned off the proud-flesh. It was a long hour. To alleviate some of the pain, I ran back and forth between the ship's stern and bow until I was pooped, and my arm had cooled off.

San Diego and Coronado

On 18 November, our first sight of land was San Clemente Island, a thrilling sight. Shortly after, the *Lurliner* approached the entrance to San Diego Bay. We entered the harbor, and the *Lurliner* was docked at the downtown Navy Pier. I disembarked from the *Lurliner* carrying all my worldly possessions in a brown paper sack: a pair of boxer shorts made in Kobe, Japan, courtesy of a *Lurliner's* officer; toilet articles, flight suit, helmet, goggles, yellow life jacket, 45-caliber gun and a Naval Institute magazine. I was traveling light. I was transported in a station wagon to the San Diego Balboa Naval Hospital.

The Navy Wives Communication System

That same day, a Navy wife called Annie and told her I was aboard the *Lurliner* that had just docked. Back on 14 November, Annie had received a one-star Western Union telegram informing her I had been wounded in action. A two-star telegram in WWII meant you were killed. Here is Annie's story of the events in her life as a Navy wife who was worried about me after hearing on the radio there had been a major carrier battle in the South Pacific:

In May, I had returned to my mother's home in Iowa to be with her. She was now in the latter stages of terminal cancer. Mail from the Hornet was sporadic and further and further apart. From the latter part of August to the end of September, there was no mail until I received a letter the day of my mother's funeral. She had been in a coma before she died, but she came out of the coma for a short moment, held my hand, and patted it as she told me, "Don't cry honey, he will come home." Then she took her last breath.

There was no mail until 14 November after I had returned to Coronado. Just after I had arrived, tired from driving all day, there was a message from the Western Union's office in the Hotel del Coronado to call their office. Getting up the courage to call, trembling and crying because I expected the worst, I asked them to read the message. They said, "Is someone with you?" The wife of a squadron pilot was with me so they agreed to deliver the message to me:

THE NAVY DEPARTMENT DEEPLY REGRETS TO INFORM YOU THAT LIEUTENANT JUNIOR GRADE CLAYTON EVAN FISHER US NAVAL RESERVE HAS BEEN WOUNDED IN ACTION IN THE PERFORMANCE OF HIS DUTY AND IN THE SERVICE OF HIS COUNTRY X THE DEPARTMENT APPRECIATES YOUR GREAT ANXIETY AND WILL FURNISH YOU FURTHER INFORMATION PROMPLY WHEN RECEIVED X TO PREVENT POSSIBLE AID TO OUR ENEMIES PLEASE DO NO NOT DIVULGE THE NAME OF HIS SHIP OR STATION.

On November 18th I was distraught and walked to the beach in Coronado, sat on a bench looking out over the ocean and trying to sort out my thoughts of what should I do next. After returning to my apartment, I received a phone call from another squadron pilot's wife that took me out of my depression to exhilaration. She told me she thought my husband was aboard the Lurliner which had docked that morning at the Navy Pier in San Diego. Then my next thoughts were, how bad is he wounded and what will he look like?

The rest of the day I made repeated calls to the San Diego Balboa Naval Hospital to get information about him. Always the same answer, he is not listed on our admission records. Finally at 4:00 pm, there was a LTJG Clayton Fisher on the records. Of course, I wanted to get to the hospital as soon as possible and I asked about visiting hours. The hours were over but they told me I could visit at any time. Grabbing my car keys – I was out the door – and on my way.

I shared a hospital room with another pilot from the *Hornet*. We decided to walk to downtown San Diego to see what the city lights looked like. We didn't have uniforms or money. I had on blue sailor dungarees and a khaki shirt. Leaving our room, I noticed a Navy corpsman coming down the corridor escorting a young woman. He mentioned my name, and I realized the woman was Annie. This was an extremely emotional reunion. Forget the city lights! Annie and I drove over to Coronado to the rented apartment that she shared with another squadron pilot's wife. A week later when her husband returned, the partying began. When the music and partying got too loud, the landlord, who resided below the apartment, would bang on the ceiling with a broom handle to quiet things down.

Identification Card

When I had first arrived at San Diego Balboa Naval Hospital, I didn't have an identification card. You needed one to get onto North Island Air Station so that Annie and I could visit the Officer's Club for evening meals. I was told it would take a few days to get one, but if I wanted to speed things up, I could go downtown to the Navy Federal building to get my ID. When I got there, I was stopped at the door when the security guard wanted to see my ID. After some bickering, the guard agreed to escort me to the ID office. Behind the desk was a retired Navy commander who'd been ordered back to active duty. He berated me for being negligent in losing my ID card. I explained I was a *Hornet* naval-aviator survivor, and we only wore our dog tags while flying. He undid his collar and showed me his ID attached to a plastic cord hanging around his neck. I told him it was a great innovation, but impractical for combat ships. The searing heat from bomb blasts caused most of the *Hornet's* casualties. The heat imbedded finger rings and small metal chains holding dog tags into burned flesh. Plastic cords would melt and burn.

Uniform Reimbursement

Officers are required to buy their own uniforms. When you lose all your uniforms and clothes, you don't realize how many items you've lost until you make a list of them. A naval aviation officer has four basic uniforms: blue, white, khaki and aviation green. Now, add all the accessories, ties, shirts, belts, gloves, shoes, stockings and caps with all the different colors. Next, add blue and tan raincoats, rank insignia and aviators gold wings. The government would reimburse us for our uniforms loss, but not personal items like watches.

At 1942 money values, I estimated the cost to replace my uniforms and underclothing to be about seven-hundred dollars. The survivor claims were administered at the Navy's Federal Building. Again, another recalled retired commander initially interviewed me. One of his first statements was about *Yorktown* survivor claims he had processed. He told me, "I'm not going to let you *Hornet* survivors screw the government like the *Yorktown* survivors did on their claims." I couldn't believe what I was hearing; I wanted to tell him what an asshole he was, but thought better, because he'd be processing my claim. After submitting a claim for $700, the claim was reduced to $475. My uniforms ended up costing me nearly a thousand dollars which I had to pay on an installment plan.

Thirty Days Convalescent Leave

My arm wound had healed and I was given thirty days leave before receiving orders back to active duty. Annie and I were going to travel to my home and be with my family for the Christmas holidays. We took the famous old train, the *Challenger,* from Los Angeles to Chicago. Shortly after boarding, I met a ship's naval officer who had just returned from the South Pacific. He told me news that had not officially been released to the press. The *Juneau* had been badly damaged in night-surface action with Japanese battleships off Guadalcanal. The ship was "finished off" when she was blown up and sunk with all hands by a torpedo fired from a Japanese submarine *I-26* just south of Guadalcanal. It was terrible shocking news. Captain Swenson, who had endangered his ship and crew to rescue me and my gunner, and Dr. Neff, who treated us, were both dead. Years later, I found out there were only ten *Juneau* survivors out of approximately 117 crew members who had survived the torpedo's explosion. It was a horrible death for some of the men; they were attacked and eaten by sharks.

The train's passengers were mostly servicemen. The first time Annie and I tried to enter the dining car the attendant told me, "We only serve men in uniform." I grabbed Annie by the hand and told the attendant, "This is my wife, and she is coming in the diner with me!" After pushing by the attendant, I dragged Annie by her hand, into the diner. That ended the problem for the remainder of the trip. The trip was going to take four days, and our train was sidetracked frequently to allow troop and supply trains to continue west. We ate Spam for breakfast the last morning before arriving in Chicago. We then had lunch at the Palmer House Hotel and splurged with two orders of large servings of shrimp salad.

After arriving home, I again became reacquainted again with my dog, Peter. Now that I had become somewhat of a hometown celebrity, our local newspaper wanted my picture. After making a deal with the photographer, he agreed to take my picture including my family and dog in the photo. Better yet, the photo had Annie, her fingers sticking through the shrapnel holes in my flight suit.

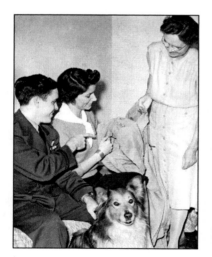

Shrapnel holes in flight suit - my mother Eva Fisher, Annie, my dog Peter and myself – Photo courtesy of the Janesville Gazette.

All my friends were gone. They either had volunteered or had been drafted in the military service. Being the first serviceman that had been wounded in combat to get back to my hometown, the Rotary, Kiwanis and a YMCA social club all asked me to be their guest speaker. Friends of my mother dropped by uninvited and wanted to hear about my war experience. I felt it was an intrusion on my personal privacy, and to this day, I value my privacy and don't envy the various movie and athletic celebrities.

After retuning to San Diego, I was discharged from the hospital with a Purple Heart and orders to the Operational Flight Training Command at NAS Jacksonville, Florida.

CHAPTER 16
NAVAL AIR STATION
FORT LAUDERDALE

Annie and I drove across country to Jacksonville with all our worldly possessions in the trunk and back seat of our old Buick sedan. War rationing of many items like gasoline, tires, foods like meat and sugar was now in effect. Fortunately, I had bought a new set of tires before the attack on Pearl Harbor because now many factories had switched over to only manufacturing war materials. As we traveled, we stopped frequently in small towns off the main highways to try and buy an alarm clock, toaster and electric flat iron. The stores were empty of all appliances. In Austin, Texas, we spotted a single toaster sitting in a display window of a department store. The store was closed for the night, but the next morning, we eagerly waited for it to open. Yes, the toaster was for sale, and we smugly carried our trophy out of the store.

The previous afternoon as we were approaching Austin, Annie was thumbing through the latest issue of *Life,* which was the most popular magazine during the war. Showing me a page in the magazine of a group of individual pictures of unidentified Army Air Corps aircrew members, she pointed at one of the pictures and asked me, "Who do you think this picture looks like?" I was driving, glanced at the picture and said, "Maybe it looks a little like me." This issue of *Life* magazine had a cover story about Captain Eddie Rickenbacker, a famous WWI fighter plane ace. He'd been aboard a *B-17* that had departed Hickman Field in Honolulu, and because of poor navigation, they failed to find Tahiti, their destination. The plane ran out of fuel, and they were forced to ditch into the water. Rickenbacker and the crew spent twenty-some days in their life rafts. Rickenbacker was being paid for the story and decided to donate the money to an Airman's Relief Fund. After switching seats and while Annie was driving, I examined the photo and told her, "Hell Annie, that picture is me!"

A *Life* magazine photo editor had mistakenly pulled my picture from their photo archives thinking I was an Army Air Corps air crewman. The photograph was the one taken of me in the cockpit of my plane by a *Life* photographer at Columbia, S.C. in November of 1941. The type of Navy flight helmet and the fur-collared flight jacket I was wearing made it possible for me to identify myself. No one else could. I liked telling my friends that I had made it into *Life* magazine. Who cared if I was a nameless pilot?

Ensign Fisher - Army maneuvers South Carolina
November 1941- LIFE photo

After reporting to Jacksonville Air Station, I received orders to the Naval Air Station Fort Lauderdale to train and qualify as a LSO. When qualified, the new LSOs would be assigned to new aircraft carriers as they reached the fleet.

My first training was with a group of future LSOs conducting FCLP with pilots that had recently finished carrier operational flight training. The pilots were flying the North American *SNJ* trainer, which I had flown in my basic-stage flight training. During our instruction, we stood behind an experienced qualified LSO and observed him executing signals to the incoming plane.

Sometimes, we had three or four student LSO's standing in line behind the LSO and we took turns guiding the planes. It was like the blind leading the blind. You had to be alert and never take your eyes off the incoming plane. The worst situation was a pilot not responding to slow signals. The plane could stall out and spin into the ground in front of us. I learned quickly to know when to run laterally to clear the area where the plane might crash. Being an old track star in college, I usually was the fastest novice LSO to clear the danger area.

After qualifying as a LSO at Opa Locke, Miami, I returned to Fort Lauderdale to conduct FCLP at a small outlying airfield. Fort Lauderdale was an operational training base for the new Grumman *TBF* torpedo bomber. It was scary when I worked my first *TBF*, it looked so big and slow coming toward me. If the plane slowed down too much, the left wing would drop, drag along the ground and swerve right toward the LSO's position.

Sometimes you had to make a quick decision about whether to run right or left. There were a couple incidents where a LSO was injured or killed, but, thankfully, the accident rate was very low. As I gained experience, I found it rewarding to have the student pilots riding mostly roger signals and taking the cut signal for a good landing.

HOOKED

Torpedo bomber - Pilot has taken cut signal from the LSO
U.S. Navy photo

While conducting FCLP at an outlying field, we had periods of time between flights. To overcome boredom, we decided to do FCLP with a Piper *Cub* we used for transportation. One LSO would fly the *Cub* in a miniature flight pattern. We approached the LSO flying at a twenty-foot altitude and just above the *Cub's* stalling speed. We could control the speed and altitude by slightly moving the throttle with the tip of our finger. At the cut signal, the *Cub* would drop hard to the runway. We had to stop doing FCLP because the leaf spring that supported the tail wheel would hit the bottom of the rudder and bend its frame.

LT Cason, a friend and former squadron pilot, was also an LSO stationed at NAS Opa Locke. We'd fly Piper *Cubs* and *SNJ's* for transportation to outlying fields to conduct FCLP. My friend loved to fly up to the outlying field where I was working and try to chase me off the runway with his *SNJ*. At times, he'd fly so low, I'd have to dive for cover under a crash truck. He never let up. When I was flying the *Cub,* he'd come from behind, chase me and try to dogfight. I was at a disadvantage, because he had more visibility from the *SNJ* than I did from the *Cub*. His antics were becoming too hairy, so one day, I decided to start my engine first for takeoff and fly low over the trees heading for Fort Lauderdale, hoping Cason couldn't catch up. Normally, I got in the *Cub* started the engine and waited for someone to pull my wheel chocks. To fool Cason, I kicked the chocks away from the wheels, reached through the open door, turned the engine switch on and slightly advanced the throttle. Then putting my left foot in front of the right wheel, I reached forward with my right arm to grab a propeller blade from the backside and sharply pulled it down to start the engine. With the engine running, the plane moved slowly forward, I climbed in the seat and was ready to takeoff. Cason was cranking up the inertia starter on his plane, when he realized I was beating him. He jumped off the wing, ran over, and sat on the right wing spar of the *Cub*. He told me to takeoff, and I told him to get the hell off the wing strut. Next, he crawled up on the back of the *Cub* near its tail and again told me to take off. I was getting tired of the little game and decided to scare Cason, so I added a little engine throttle and started slowly rolling down the runway. I intended to slightly bounce the front wheels. However, with Cason's weight on the tail, the *Cub's* front wheels lifted off the runway with the tail wheel still rolling on the runway, and I'm looking up at blue sky! I chopped the throttle, and when the wheels hit the runway, the right, landing-wheel axle bent, and the tire blew out. A landing-gear strut and wheel assembly were taken off another Cub at the air station and installed on my *Cub,* and I flew it back to NAS Fort Lauderdale. Cason never heckled me again.

The Cub became a "hanger queen" for a couple weeks with the right axle sitting on a sawhorse. It needed a new inner tube for the tire which had to be ordered through the supply department. Everyday, I looked at that forlorn *Cub* hoping that damn inner tube would arrive soon. So far, nobody had questioned me about this little fiasco, until one day while I was standing on the hanger mezzanine, my boss CDR Taylor (C.O. VT-5 aboard the *Yorktown* during the Coral Sea battle) looking down at the *Cub,* asked me, "Fisher, just what in the hell were you doing with that *Cub*?" I said, "Commander, I'll never tell." He just laughed. I had just received orders to NAS Glenview and was checking out with him. End of story.

Annie became pregnant after we arrived at Fort Lauderdale. She was extremely nauseated during her third month and was hospitalized. At that time, the doctors didn't know her problem was from a hormone imbalance. I had received orders to NAS Glenview, Illinois, to be an LSO on the aircraft training carriers operating in Lake Michigan. My mother had arrived in Fort Lauderdale to help me take care of Annie and to accompany and assist her to travel by train to my home. In the mean time, Annie's doctor decided she should have a blood transfusion because of her weakened condition. LT Muery, who had attended our wedding and survived 24 days in a life raft, was now also stationed at NAS Fort Lauderdale. He had the same blood type as Annie and volunteered to donate blood. Shortly after the blood transfusion, miraculously, the nausea stopped. She was now on her feet and could travel.

CHAPTER 17
LAKE MICHIGAN - AIRCRAFT TRAINING CARRIERS

USS Wolverine and USS Sable

Hundreds of Naval Aviators needed to be carrier qualified for the new carrier air groups being formed for the many new aircraft carriers that had been built. Due to the German submarine menace in the Atlantic Ocean and lack of small carriers suitable for carrier qualifying pilots, two coal-burning, side-wheeler *Great Lakes* excursion boats were converted in 1941 to aircraft training carriers. The boats were renamed the *USS Wolverine* and *USS Sable.* The carriers operated in Lake Michigan and docked at the Navy Pier in Chicago.

USS Wolverine & USS Sable - harbor next to Navy Pier - U.S. Navy photo

USS Wolverine on Lake Michigan - U.S. Navy photo

Aviators ordered from their operational training units to fleet squadrons had temporary duty orders to the Carrier Qualification Training Unit based at NAS Glenview, Illinois. The procedure for pilots checking in and out of the Training Unit was streamlined from the normal and traditional system.

The procedure was centralized and conducted in an aircraft hanger. The pilot's orders were processed, medical records checked, pay accounts serviced, and wartime gasoline ration coupons issued. It was possible for a pilot on the same day to check into the Training Unit, take refresher FCLP, become carrier qualified and then check out with his orders to his Fleet squadron. Usually it took three days to process a pilot through the system; however, weather could be a big obstacle, extending the process.

The pilot's flew the same aircraft for the refresher field-carrier landings that they would be flying in their fleet squadrons. The pilots had to make a minimum of six landings to qualify. The reason some pilots failed to qualify was usually due to a mental problem, mostly fear. For pilots to master carrier landings, there was a cost. There were some fatalities, and a lot of lost aircraft. Today, there are over 100 planes resting on the bottom of Lake Michigan.

F4F Wildcat fighter spinning and crashing off bow of carrier –
U.S. Navy photo

During the period of June and July, I worked as an LSO on both the *Wolverine* and *Sable.* A maximum effort was underway to work off a large backlog of pilots, due to prolonged bad weather and an increase in new arrivals from the operational training units. As a result, competition between the carriers quickly developed to qualify the most pilots per day. The *Sable* set a new record in July by qualifying over sixty pilots in a single day. I was a member of the team of LSOs that worked that day. We landed our first aircraft as soon as there was enough daylight that morning and finished with the last aircraft as the ship approached the Navy Pier at dusk. The flight deck crew did a superb job as each plane landed. The crew then pushed the plane back to the stern, so there would be enough space for the plane to be able to take off and circle the ship for another landing. It was a very long day. On our last aircraft flight that day, the flight pattern extended from the ship to Chicago's Michigan Avenue. The *F4F Wildcat* fighters that were in the flight pattern made a good show for the commuter traffic that came to a standstill to watch the operation.

Our senior LSO was LT Peters who had been the LSO on the *Hornet* until she was sunk 27 October 1942. The other LSO's and I had about four months experience working mostly *F4F* fighters and the *TBF* torpedo bombers doing FCLP in Florida. After a few days on the *Wolverine* and *Sable,* you became an experienced LSO in a hurry.

Lake Michigan is about sixty miles wide east of Chicago. As prevailing winds were usually from west to east, the operating area for the carriers was limited. The carriers usually had to steam across the lake before turning into the wind for flight operations.

One day during flight operations, an excursion boat steamed along close to the *Wolverine's* starboard side. It crowded in for a better view, so its passengers could watch the flight operations. The passengers were waving at us, and our sailors were waving back. The only unhappy person on the *Wolverine* was the captain; he kept screaming over a bull horn at the excursion boat to pull away.

What I remember most about the *Great Lakes* carrier operations was how cold it could be on the flight deck in June and how burnt coal cinders continually got into your eyes. Being on the portside aft, the location of the LSO platform was about the worst position on the ship because the gases from the smokestack containing soot and cinders continuously flowed over it. We all wore aviation goggles with vent holes that prevented fogging, but those vents, unfortunately, were the perfect entry for the airborne cinders. The LSO's always had soot on their faces and flight jackets, and they periodically had to have cinders removed from their eyes.

LSO's would often lead small formations of aircraft flown by students from the Glenview air station to the carriers. As flight leader on my first flight, I received the "Peter Charley" radio signal from the carrier (the phonetic successor of "Prep Cast" used in the Navy in 1942) which I assumed was the signal to start landing. Feeling a little cocky, I smartly broke the formation to start a carrier approach. Due to the enemy submarine threat during my 1942 *Hornet* tour, our flight leaders, on receiving a blinker Prep Cast signal, immediately broke formation and started downwind to minimize the amount of time the *Hornet* was committed to a steady course. However, the fresh water Navy used "Peter Charley" as a preparatory command and "Charley" as the command of execution. As I was making what I thought was a great final approach and expecting to start getting a roger, the *Wolverine* started turning 90 degrees to starboard. As I aborted my landing approach, my student pilots, who had been flying downwind in the landing pattern, were now milling around in confusion all over the south end of Lake Michigan. As I attempted to get the pilots back in formation, it was like herding cats. Amidst all the chaos, I was getting a real butt-chewing from the ship's captain. This wasn't one of my proudest moments as the operation was cancelled.

Carrier qualification operations are always a little hairy due to the limited flight experience of the pilots. On one occasion, I repeatedly had to wave off a *TBF* pilot who was not responding to my "fast" signals. He was just too fast in his final approach. Finally, I asked LT Peters, who had been the LSO on the *Hornet,* to take over. Peters had to give the pilot two more waves-offs. He finally gave the pilot a roger and then a cut signal. The pilot cut his throttle, just as the plane was settling to the flight deck he panicked, pulled back hard on the control stick and jammed on full throttle. The plane floated nose high above the deck, cleared the crash barrier, drifted over the ship's bridge and tore most of the right wing off when it hit the steel pipe tripod mast.

The ship's captain and other personnel standing on the bridge narrowly missed being injured or killed. The plane then rolled over on its back and struck the water. The plane floated with its landing gear sticking up; the pilot never got out of the cockpit. The plane was recovered the next morning along with the pilot's body. His neck had been broken. The night before the fatal crash, I had stayed aboard the *Wolverine* along with some student pilots. The deceased pilot had been assigned a bunk just above mine. After he got in his bunk, he had started complaining about how uncomfortable his bunk was. I told him, "I think you can survive one night aboard ship, so stop bitching."

147

HOOKED

Missing the Ship a Serious Offense in the Navy

I was assigned duty as LSO on the *Wolverine,* to wave aboard a TBF plane the next morning with a team of LSO's who were to conduct carrier landings that day. Annie and I had rented a bedroom in Northwestern University Music Conservatory in the city of Evanston just north of Chicago. We still hadn't been able to buy an alarm clock so after over sleeping, I hurriedly struggled into my uniform, jumped in my car and headed for the Navy Pier, crawling along at 35-mph, which was the wartime speed limit and was strictly enforced.

As I approached the dock, the *Wolverine* had just pulled away. Missing your ship in wartime could be a court-martial offense. Driving back to Glenview, I knew I'd screwed up the ship's operations for that day. After reporting to the air operations officer at Glenview and telling him my sad story, he said, "Fisher you're lucky! One of our LSOs had decided to go aboard the evening before." Grinning at me, he continued, "Fisher, you're not down in the Florida vacation land, you're back in the fleet," meaning, the *Wolverine* and the *Sable* were the fleet!

On days not assigned to the carriers, the LSOs conducted FCLP on a grass-covered field a few miles northwest of the Glenview air station. It was tedious work and sometimes nerve-racking. Working the fighters was tricky, and I had one crash in front of me. One morning, while riding in a station wagon with a group of LSO's and approaching the gate to the practice field, a fighter plane crashed through a fence into the adjacent cornfield parallel to us, cut a long swath through the corn stalks, and nosed up as it finally came to a halt. What a way to start the day. It's no wonder that I recently had a vivid nightmare where I was standing in the middle of Northwestern University's football field in Dyke Stadium with planes continuously zooming low over my head.

By the end of July, I anxiously awaited orders to a fleet carrier and was completely surprised to receive orders to NAS Vero Beach, an operational training base for dive bombers. Later, I found out that CDR Taylor, my previous boss at NAS Fort Lauderdale, was concerned about the seriousness of Anne's medical condition. He had requested the Bureau of Naval Personnel to reassign me to an operational training command billet in Florida. His request was accepted, and I received orders to NAS Vero Beach to be a dive-- bomber instructor.

CHAPTER 18
NAVAL AIR STATION VERO BEACH

The air station at Vero Beach, Florida's sole mission was to train dive-bomber pilots. Other new temporary wartime air stations training carrier pilots were Daytona Beach, Orlando, Melbourne and Fort Lauderdale. These air stations provided carrier operational flight training in fighters, dive bombers and torpedo bombers. All the flight students were naval officers as well as some British naval officers who had previously completed flight training. The operational flight training was intense, thorough, and supervised mostly by combat experienced flight instructors. Unless delayed by weather, flight training was conducted seven days a week. There was no time for the traditional Navy's weekly personnel and administrative inspections.

The dive-bomber aircraft flown at Vero Beach were the Brewster *SB2A Buccaneers.* The Dutch government had originally purchased the planes but never received the planes because Holland had been overrun and was occupied by the German army; consequently, our navy accepted them. All the flight and power instruments were configured using metric system numbers and Dutch words. Narrow pieces of red tape were pasted on the glass faces of the instruments to indicate the acceptable range of temperatures, pressures etc. The *SB2A* was too "hot" for carrier landings and would spin in just under 85 knots in a landing approach. The plane was a great "diver" and very steady; you felt as if you were flying down a railroad track.

Custer's Wild Ride

In one of my flight classes, I had a student named Ensign Custer who was just too scared to take his plane into a dive any steeper than 50 degrees. This problem became a challenge for me. One day, out of desperation with him, I drove a radio-equipped *Jeep* out onto Tampa Road, west of Vero Beach, and marked out a huge white "X" on the road surface to be used as target. Then using the *Jeep's* radio, I tried to talk Custer into "steepening" his dive up to 70 degrees so that he could experience and know the sensation and, maybe, heighten his sense of the perimeters. He just would not take the plane over 55 degrees and always pulled out way too early in his dives. My last resort was to take Custer up in the rear cockpit of a dive bomber and have him experience the feel of a 70-degree dive. Either he would break through his fear and become a qualified dive bomber, or he would be transferred out of the dive-bomber training program. I took the plane up to 12,000 feet and then entered a 70-degree dive on a target boat at sea. Judging your altitude changes while diving on a target boat is more difficult than on a land target where you notice differences in the size of trees and other objects on the ground. As soon as I reached 70 degrees in my dive, Custer panicked and screamed at me over the radio all the way down, so I deliberately made a low pullout of the dive. After flying back to the air station, I set up my landing approach downwind, and then I angrily jammed the landing-gear handle down to lower the wheels. As I watched the landing-gear indicators, only the left wheel dropped and locked in the "down" position. The day had now drastically changed for the two of us!

Each time I retracted the wheel that was down, and tried again to lower both wheels, the right wheel still hung up, and the wheel indicator just wiggled. After pulling up to 3,000 feet to clear the other air traffic around the field, I tried using the emergency release procedure to drop the hung wheel to no avail. The wheels on the dive bomber had an extremely widespread landing gear, and the wheel struts had to be compressed to allow the wheels to clear indentations in the sides of the fuselage. The actuating lever fastened to the right strut had failed. Without the strut compressing, the wheel would jiggle but could not move down. Without knowing that the wheel was mechanically unable to drop, I kept trying to resolve the problem by jerking the nose of the plane up violently hoping to jar the wheel loose, but the wheel indicator did not change. The senior flight-training officer was in the control tower giving me various gems of advice. Frankly, I wasn't too concerned about landing; all I had to do was retract the down wheel and land the plane with the wheels up. He wanted me to try and bounce the down wheel on the runway as I was flying down the runway. He practically ordered me to do what I considered to be a dangerous maneuver. With the plane's extremely wide landing gear, I could easily drag a wing tip and possibly cartwheel the plane and crash.

In the mean time, Annie, who was almost due to deliver our first child, had gone out to the air-station dispensary for a check up with her doctor who was also a flight surgeon. She met him just as he was rushing out of the dispensary to an ambulance waiting to take him to a standby position on the runway. She knew I was flying and hoped I was not the pilot involved. Annie frantically said to the surgeon, "Jim, don't let it be Clayton." He replied, "Oh, it's not him. It won't be him."

She decided to drive down toward the hanger area to see what was going on. Sailors were sitting on the hanger roof waiting for the action that most likely would ensue on the airfield. To satisfy the senior-flight instructor in the control tower, I decided I'd make a landing approach and just roll the one wheel on the runway. The plane had a "standpipe" in the main fuel tank, so you could switch a gas valve to either feed fuel from the bottom of the tank or to feed it from the top of the standpipe. The fuel below the top of the standpipe was reserve fuel. I switched the valve to feed fuel from the bottom of the tank before making the landing approach. After touching the wheel on the runway and rolling on it a short distance, I immediately aborted the maneuver and climbed to 1,500 feet before switching back to feed fuel above the top of the standpipe. The engine started cutting out, so I hurriedly switched back to the bottom of the main tank. Thankfully, my engine started again.

Now I had a serious problem. How much reserve fuel below the top

153

of the standpipe had I used? I retracted the down left wheel, called the control tower to declare an emergency, and then stated that I had to land immediately with my wheels up. They wanted me to delay my landing until they could get a LSO out to the head of the runway to direct me in on a carrier-type landing approach to land. Doing that, I would be flying slow and low barely over the tops of some pine trees before turning for my final approach to the runway. Ignoring the advice from the control tower, I positioned myself at 1,500 feet to begin the downwind leg of my landing pattern feeling confident that I could make a safe wheels-up landing on or off the runway. Fortunately, just as I was flying by the control tower at 1,500 feet, my engine quit. I was out of fuel. After quickly lowering my landing flaps, I managed to complete a 180-degree turn into the wind; however, as I was making the last 90 degrees of my turn, it appeared to the crash and ambulance crews that the plane was headed right at their vehicles. There was a mad scramble for every body to get clear of the vehicles. The plane skidded to a stop adjacent to the ambulance and the crash truck stationed on the edge of the runway. During the chaos, the flight surgeon was banged up, and ended up with a badly bruised leg. In all the commotion as Custer and I climbed out of the plane, I don't remember even talking to him. Ensign Custer had a wild ride that day, one that he probably would never forget.

SB2A Brewster dive bomber - emergency wheels-up landing
U.S. Navy photo

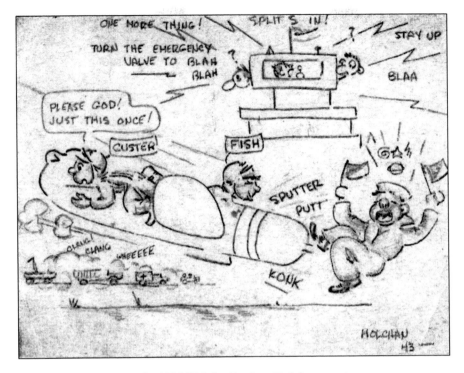

'Custer's Wild Ride' - Ensign Holchan cartoon

Ensign Holchan, a fellow student of Ensign Custer, sketched a humorous cartoon depicting the ordeal and presented it to me as a gift during a pilot's briefing. We all had a good laugh.

Annie had watched me land the plane, but she didn't know I was the pilot and returned to the dispensary. Finally the flight surgeon, with his gimpy leg, returned to the dispensary, grabbed Annie and said, "Annie that was your husband in that plane and he's all right!" This flight surgeon attended Annie when she delivered our first daughter on 19 November.

There was a joke among the pilots' wives at Vero Beach about the number of them that were pregnant at the same time. Maybe pregnancy was contagious? Anyway, Annie was due to deliver in the middle of the month along with two other gals. One of the two was "Connie" Mason, the daughter-in-law of Admiral Mason, who had been in command of the *USS Hornet* when the carrier was sunk during the Battle of Santa Cruz. Connie's husband, LCDR "Charley" Mason, Jr, was training as a dive-bomber pilot. "Peggy" Iverson, the other pregnant wife, was married to Marine Major "Danny" Iverson, who was a dive-bomber flight instructor. He had survived the battle of Midway flying a *SBD* dive bomber. His plane was badly damaged, riddled with 219 bullet holes, but he was still able to make it back and land at Midway. Only a few pilots in his squadron survived the battle. From Midway he was transferred to Henderson Field at Guadalcanal to fly dive bombers. The airfield was named in memory of a Marine squadron commander who was killed during the Midway battle. Attempting to neutralize the airfield for flight operations at night, the Japanese battleships fired numerous rounds of high-explosive shells at Henderson Field. It was a terrifying experience for all the air-support personnel and the pilots. The only shelters were fairly shallow trenches and fox holes, but they were no protection from a close or direct hit. Danny survived that ordeal and finally was ordered to Vero Beach.

The three gals who were expecting were attended to and had their babies delivered on schedule by our flight surgeon at the Fort Pierce County Hospital. During the war, most of the younger doctors had been drafted into military service. Charley Mason, Danny Iverson and I drove to the hospital each evening to see the new mamas and their babies. We proud papas carried the babies to each mother's room to show them off. Connie had a boy, Peggy and Annie both had girls. Annie's little prize was a red head we named Susan.

A few days after the gals were released from the hospital, Peggy and Annie drove to Palm Beach to get the "works" at the Elizabeth Arden Salon - hair cutting, styling, and nails. This was a real wartime treat and moral builder for those gals. Annie finally confessed years later that her bill was seventy-five dollars. Imagine what that cost would be in today's dollar value. Then, a few days later, tragedy struck — an event that shocked us all. Danny was killed in a mid-air collision with one of his student pilots. One more tragedy loomed in the future. Charley Mason, after finishing his flight training at Vero Beach, became a dive-bomber squadron commander. The squadron was stationed and training at Fallon, Nevada. Charley was killed in a dive-bombing accident.

The *SBD* dive bomber that Danny Iverson flew during the Battle of Midway was returned to the States, overhauled and then returned back to service. While the plane was being flown off one of the training carriers in Lake Michigan, it crashed in the lake. The plane was recovered from the lake, restored and now is on display in the National Museum of Naval Aviation at Pensacola, Florida.

Naval Air Station Melbourne December 1943

The operational fighter training base at NAS Melbourne for *F6F Hellcat* fighters had been directed to accelerate their flight-training schedule to turn out an additional 1,500 fighter pilots as soon as possible. Flight instructors at Vero Beach were asked to volunteer for temporary assignment to Melbourne as fighter pilot instructors. In the Navy, there's an old saying, "Never volunteer." I volunteered to accept temporary assignment to Melbourne. After two years as a dive-bomber flight instructor, I expected orders back to the fleet in a dive-bomber squadron. This was my chance to be assigned to a fighter squadron rather than a dive-bomber squadron if I had enough flight experience in the *Hellcat*.

Each day I commuted to Melbourne, flying a dive-bomber plane from Vero Beach to Melbourne. After landing, I would run over to a student ready room to brief my assigned flight students. All of the training flights I instructed were focused on aerial gunnery geared to teach deflection shooting at towed cloth-target sleeves. We used gunnery lanes five to ten miles at sea off the coastline of Florida.

A fighter plane was set up with a towline attached to its tail, with the line and sleeve parallel to the runway and the full length of the line of the target sleeve ahead of the plane. The tow pilot held the plane's brakes, lowered his landing flaps and added full engine power. As soon as the plane got airborne, the pilot had to pull the plane's nose up sharply in order to quickly gain altitude and snatch the sleeve off the ground so as not to damage it by dragging it on the runway. This was a dangerous maneuver; your plane could stall out if your engine quit. After the training flight, the tow pilot flew over a drop zone and released the sleeve which would later be marked and the bullet holes counted. The plane's fifty-caliber guns ammunition had the tips of each bullet dipped in different colored paint. When the painted bullet punched a hole in the sleeve, it left a colored mark, so we were able to determine the number of hits each pilot got in the target sleeve.

In one of my flight classes, I had two pilots that were not getting enough hits on the target sleeves, and there was some concern about qualifying them as combat fighter pilots. Eventually, the two pilots received orders to combat fighter squadrons. In a *LIFE* magazine article published early in 1945, there were photographs of Navy fighter pilots who had shot down five or more Japanese planes to become "aces." One of those pilots was a flight student I had at Melbourne. Later, I met him at Vero Beach, and I asked him how he became an ace. He just laughed and told me, "We didn't have to do any deflection shooting; we got directly behind them and blasted away. In fact, we almost had to take turns as to who was going to shoot the poor bastard's plane down."

The Melbourne fighter planes at that time were very dirty due to oily exhaust gases from the engines that spread along the bottom and sides of the fuselages which, in turn, attracted a lot of dust and dirt. It seemed like the ground maintenance crews only had time to refuel and load ammo for the fifty-caliber guns and none to clean the planes. Each plane was scheduled for six flights per day, and the ground crews and planes were being pushed to their limits. Flight safety didn't have the highest priority in those wartime accelerated flight-training programs. Once, I heard the student fatality rate at Melbourne was about one pilot for every 1,000 hours flight training in 1943.

One afternoon, I was "chasing students" on my third flight to do eight overhead, full-deflection gunnery runs. On each run after firing at the sleeve, the pilot pulled "Gs" while recovering from the maneuver, and then he climbed up to get back in formation. Pulling "Gs" was physically tiring for the pilot especially after making multiple gunnery runs.

After you completed your gunnery run, you had to be very aware of the position of the plane that had completed the gunnery run ahead of you. If the pilot ahead of you had been slow in recovering from his run he could be above and behind your position as he was closing his distance to rejoin the formation. This situation was a perfect setup for a mid-air collision. If you were looking up at the formation, unaware of the other planes, you could be climbing up underneath a lagging plane. Also, your plane could be in a blind spot under the other pilot's wings. We drilled into our students, "Count the planes!" In an eight-plane formation as you recovered from your run, you should be able to count seven planes. Your plane should always be number eight.

I'm Going to Get Wet!

During the last gunnery run we were making that afternoon, one pilot got out of the normal position and was too far behind the formation, and I had chewed him out. Then when I made my run, I also became too steep in the run and was out of position. To avoid embarrassment and quickly get back into my formation, I pushed my throttle full forward for maximum power. With no warning, the engine just plain quit. Pulling full power on every takeoff was standard procedure, so I wasn't abusing the engine.

Our flight was about ten miles due east of Melbourne on the edge of the Gulf Stream. From my altitude of about 9,000 feet, the Hellcats rate of descent was about 3,000 feet per minute, so I calculated that I had about three minutes before I was going to get wet. The sea was glassy smooth. It was about 1600, and in the middle of December there was little daylight left at that hour. I decided to use only the half-down position for my landing flaps so that the flaps wouldn't dig into the water as much when the plane contacted the surface. The plane slid on the smooth water for a short distance instead of making a hard impact landing.

Water was pouring into the cockpit. I hurriedly released my seat belt and stood up to get out of my parachute harness because water had already filled the cockpit. After climbing out on the right wing and unhooking one parachute leg strap, I felt the plane starting to sink, and

I moved out farther on the wing to avoid getting dragged down by the tail. My life jacket was inflated. I struggled to get my other leg strap released, so the life raft could separate from the parachute pack. The life raft had a safety strap that was attached to the lifejacket so you wouldn't lose the raft. Single-man rafts were difficult to climb into, so I positioned the raft between my legs and pulled the toggle on the CO_2 bottle, and — presto! — I was sitting in the raft.

My adrenaline must have been working overtime while ditching the plane and getting in the raft because I was completely exhausted. Lying in the raft and just starting to relax, I started hearing a hissing sound. I almost panicked thinking that the raft was leaking! Then I noticed there were small water bubbles around the rafts emergency valve. It had a short length of rubber hose connected to the valve, and if you opened the valve, you could use your mouth and blow air into the raft. Whoever packed the raft had not fully tightened the valve, and it was leaking CO_2. There was cheesecloth wrapped around the valve to protect it, and with wet gloves, I had trouble tightening the valve shut. Finally, I fully closed the valve, but now the raft was very limp. My butt was low in the bottom of the raft, and my arms and legs were dangling over the side.

Now, I had another problem — I was floating under the gunnery lanes. As I watched a target tow plane approaching high above me, it would be passing right over me. I tried to determine whether a fighter would be firing down toward me, but as the tow plane quickly passed beyond me, I realized I was out of danger.

A single-engine seaplane — the type that was catapulted off our cruisers — flew over and circled me a couple times and then flew back toward its base. Those small aircraft do not make open sea landings, but at least my location was now known. Later I noticed a group of large yellow and reddish brown sea turtles surfacing near me. They all kept sticking their heads up and appeared to be looking at me. At least I wasn't being bothered by sharks. There were a lot of sharks lurking off the Florida coast. The thought of sharks always terrified me.

It was getting close to dusk, when a *Hellcat* fighter piloted by LT Faulkner, who had been an *Enterprise* fighter pilot during the Battle of Santa Cruz, flew over me. While circling my position, he fired tracer bullets into the water. That scared me because I didn't know what he was shooting at. Finally, I realized the tracer bullets were pointing out my position to a rescue boat from the naval amphibious base at Fort Pierce, Florida. As the rescue boat pulled up along side of me, a crew member grabbed my arms and pulled me up into the boat. It was now almost dark, and the boat's navigation lights were on. The air was colder than the water. Shivering from the cold air, I was wrapped in a blanket and given a pint of whisky. My last meal had been breakfast, and the whiskey proceeded to work its charm. By the time the boat docked, I was soused and a little rowdy.

After Annie had delivered our first daughter, she was living in a Vero Beach hotel. Other Navy wives living in the hotel knew I had ditched at sea, but didn't know I'd been rescued. The wives didn't want Annie to know I was down until they had more information. They kept visiting her room to keep her from going down to the hotel lobby and learning I had ditched somewhere in the Atlantic. Some of them were in her room when I walked in a little drunk and dragging my wet parachute pack and my deflated life raft behind me.

The duty officer at the Melbourne air station had contacted me by telephone and told me he had sent a station wagon to Fort Pierce to drive me back to Melbourne. After telling the duty officer I wanted to stay at Vero Beach that night, he ordered me to return directly to Melbourne for a medical examination. When a pilot was down, missing or killed, the medical personnel needed the pilot's medical records. Being on temporary additional duty at Melbourne, my medical records were at Vero Beach. When the medical department searched for my medical records, they found records of three flight students named Fisher, but none of the records were mine.

The station wagon dispatched from Melbourne had picked me up at the amphibious base. When we reached Vero Beach, I told the driver to drop me off at the hotel. The next morning I flew to Melbourne with my medical records and received a real first-class ass chewing from the senior flight-training officer for disobeying a direct order. He then ordered me back to Vero Beach, but not before undergoing my mandatory flight physical.

After giving my medical records to the senior flight surgeon, he wanted me to do a so-called "step-up test" with a ten-pound backpack. Still smarting from my session with the senior flight officer, I refused to do the test. The situation was getting awkward. He was a commander, and I was only a lieutenant. Then the doctor also wanted to know why my medical records were incomplete. I told him that was the medical department's problem, not mine. There was only a single page in the jacket from the *Juneau* which had been signed by Dr Neff, who had treated my arm wound after I had been rescued during the Battle of Santa Cruz. The doctor noticed doctor Neff's name and told me they'd been good friends, but he didn't know Doctor Neff had been killed. This piece of sad news neutralized the situation, and we ended up having a friendly conversation and finally shook hands.

In January 1944, NAS Vero Beach's operational training mission was changed to train fighter pilots in the *Hellcat* fighter. Our chief flight instructor decided he'd give some of the fighter pilot instructors a chance to strafe a ground gunnery target using all six of the *Hellcat's* 50-caliber guns. Normally, we only fired two guns during our aerial gunnery training flights. The target was constructed using white wooden floats arranged in a circle located in a small lake about ten miles west of the air station. The morning we checked out our individual planes for the flight, I was assigned a brand new fighter recently delivered to the air station. I read the "yellow sheet" pilots sign when they complete a flight concerning any problems or discrepancies with the aircraft. There was a notation on the yellow sheet that the pilot who had flown the standard flight acceptance test for the plane described a problem when trying to actuate the engines first-stage blower system. After another short flight test, the pilot stated the blower functioned okay.

It was a cold morning, and I ignored standard procedure of taking off with the planes canopy open and, instead, took off with the canopy closed. If the plane crashed on take off with an open canopy, there was less chance of being pinned in the cockpit. After taking off, I joined the formation in the tail-end position. Our flight leader circled the target at 6,000 feet and peeled off from the formation, and each plane followed down in a 60-degree dive. After firing my guns, recovering from my run and had reached 2,000 feet, my engine suddenly quit without any warning! A propeller blade was sticking straight up and I needed to find a spot to try and land wheels up. There was a lake on my right, large enough to glide into, but I thought about the alligators and water moccasins being in the lake and I eliminated that option. Also, I didn't want to get wet again! On my left, there was an old, abandoned, circular, dive-bombing target with a sandy emergency landing strip bisecting the target. At my altitude of 2,000 feet, it was possible to make a 180-degree turn to reach the landing strip. As I started the turn, I decided I had enough altitude to make the strip with my wheels down and save the plane. After putting my wheels down, I immediately realized it was a big mistake because I was losing altitude too fast. I tried to retract the wheels, but I didn't know they were only partially retracted. I had lost all of the hydraulic pressure because of the engine failure.

In the *Hellcat*, the landing gear struts and wheels retract into the wings; the wheels turn 90 degrees to fold flat into the bottom of the wing panels. As I continued my turn, I thought my landing gear had fully retracted, but the wheels were trailing at about a 20-degree angle with the bottom of the wings. With about the last 30 degrees left to turn, there was a tree in my path, and I lost sight of it under my right wing. It was a very bad moment until I knew I had missed the tree. When the plane slid on the sandy strip, the propeller blades bent and plowed up a lot of sand blowing it into the cockpit and hitting all over my face. As soon as the plane came to rest, I jumped out of the cockpit and ran down the right wing. The plane's radio was still on, and I could hear the other pilots talking. Nobody had missed me. Here was the chief flight instructor and five other flight instructors who were trained to keep track of their students, and they were unaware they didn't have a full formation. The radio was alive with the pilots chatter, so I climbed back on a wing grabbed the microphone and announced I was down on the landing strip. The flight leader led the formation down and buzzed me then headed back to Vero Beach.

F6F Hellcat emergency wheels-up landing - U.S. Navy photo

The cause of the engine failure was a loose nut lodged between the gears of the engine's oil pump. The nut was probably left in the engine during the previous work on the engine's blower system.

CHAPTER 19
NIGHT FIGHTER OPERATIONAL FLIGHT TRAINING

Naval Air Station Vero Beach -1944-45

In early 1944, our carrier task forces in the Pacific were harassed at night by twin-engine Japanese land-based bombers called *Bettys*. The *Bettys* were causing considerable damage to our carriers and were disrupting the sleep of the ship's crew — men who were working long, hard days supporting the daytime air combat missions. The task forces desperately needed carrier based night fighters to shoot down the *Bettys* when they were out of range of the task forces. There were few qualified carrier night-fighter pilots and aircraft with airborne intercept radar available in the task forces.

In the early spring of 1944, the training mission at Vero Beach Air Station was abruptly changed to train night-fighter pilots. They would fly newly configured Grumman *Hellcat* fighters designated as *F6F-5N* night fighter aircraft. The fighters were configured with state-of-the-art airborne intercept radar, radar-controlled gun sights, radio altimeters and red-lighted instrument panels. A senior Marine officer planned and organized the flight operations, support facilities and the necessary personnel. He had just returned from observing the Royal Air Force night-fighter operations and organization in Britain. All the night-fighter students were volunteers — pilots who had either just completed day-fighter operational training or were experienced squadron fighter pilots.

A ground radar control center was established to guide and track night fighters and target aircraft. Target aircraft were called "bogies," a word coined during WWII, meaning an unidentified aircraft. During training exercises, the bogie aircraft flew with all their external lights turned off. The radar control center, called RATC, directed the night fighters to a position where the fighter's radar could lock on to the bogie. The fighter would then fly close enough to the bogie so the pilot could get a visual contact. In an amazing short period of time, Vero Beach was now a functioning night-fighter base, with night operations commencing at 2000 and stopping at 0400 in the morning seven days a week. Initially, the old Brewster dive bombers were used as bogie targets and then replaced with the Curtis *SB2C* dive bombers called the "*Beast*." Marine pilots, Second Lieutenants, who had just finished flight school, were ordered to Vero Beach to become bogie pilots. Most of those young pilots had their dreams shattered of becoming combat fighter pilots.

The new *Hellcat F6F-5N* night fighters were slowly beginning to arrive at the base. To facilitate the training of the night fighter pilots, twin-engine *Beachcraft SNBs* aircraft were configured with identical radar as the night fighters. Flight instructors would take up two students at a time in the *SNBs*, demonstrate an interception of a bogie and be able to sight it visually. The *SNB's* were dubbed, "flying classrooms." There were not enough *F6F-5N* night fighters available for training, so a system was devised to simulate the radar interception of a bogie using a standard-configured *Hellcat fi*ghter. The fighter was directed by RATC to position it to within a night fighter's intercept-radar range of the bogie target. Next, a rear-seat observer using radio communications in the bogie plane took over by directing the fighter close enough for the fighter pilot to visually sight the blacked-out bogie plane. Those observers were called Fighter Direction Officers or FDOs.

In night-fighter training, a key factor was teaching pilots the importance of night vision. Night vision was a term used indicating your eyes had become adapted to seeing objects in very low light conditions. The student pilots attended a night-vision demonstration using a device called an Evelyn Trainer. It projected extremely low-light images on a screen in a completely dark room. As the student's eyes slowly adapted to the darkness, they started seeing slightly distinguishable silhouettes of a hanger, a vehicle, a tethered balloon, and, finally, the tethering line. Gradually, the object's silhouettes looked like a low-resolution picture. Before the classroom lights were turned on, the students would keep one eye covered. The uncovered eye felt as if it had experienced a slight electrical shock as the lights came on. With the one eye still covered and the lights turned off again, the covered eye still retained its night vision.

The air station made some major changes to facilitate pilots retaining night vision. Red lighting doesn't destroy night vision, so the pilot's ready room had red lights and the pilots wore red goggles when they left the ready room to man their planes. All the hanger windows and doors facing the parking mats had closed shutters during night flight operations. The *Hellcats* and *SNBs* had red-light instrument panels and cockpit interior lights. Special navigation maps had to be printed without using red ink because with red lighting you could not see the red ink. One night I flew a night fighter from Atlanta to Vero Beach wearing sun goggles with dark lenses with all the red interior lights turned down low until I let down to the landing flight pattern at Vero Beach. My night vision was so complete that I could see the foliage on the trees and the white strips on the runways.

The student pilots were assigned to flight wings. One wing attended ground school in the afternoon, commenced night flying at 2000 and flew until midnight. The other wing flew from midnight until 0400 then attended ground school in the morning. Breakfast was served in the officer's mess at midnight and in the mornings.

The training syllabus included: aircraft familiarization flights, night formation, night strafing on float lights dropped at sea, radar checkout, practice interceptions at high and low altitudes controlled by ground radar, airborne interceptions, very low altitude bombing using radar and a simulated "shoot down" of a bogie using radar-gun sights. The radar gun sight could lock on the bogie at a 2,000 foot range. A round dot — a radar blip — would start growing "wings" until the wing tips touched two vertical markers called "goal posts." The range to the bogie was now 1,000 feet, the shoot-down point. The *Hellcats* six 50-caliber guns were bore sighted to converge at 1,000 feet. The

Hellcat was called a "gun platform" because of the tremendous fire power of the six 50-caliber guns.

We practiced dog fighting at night utilizing the intercept mode of the fighter's radar to chase another fighter with its exterior lights turned off. It was excellent training in interpreting the movements of the bogy's blip on the radarscope and flying on instruments. You had to visualize what maneuver the bogie pilot was commencing and then match the maneuver. If you were successful, the bogy's blip would center on the scope. After gaining experience, you could usually stay on the bogie's tail.

In the two years since 1942, it amazed me how advanced the new radios and the airborne radar equipment were by 1944. To maintain the fighter's radar at peak performance, civilian electronic technicians employed by the radar manufacturers worked in our maintenance shops assisting our Navy maintenance personnel. A peaked-up radar set was used to check the replacement vacuum tubes to find defective tubes before being used in the aircraft's radar. About twenty percent of the tubes were defective and had to be discarded.

Night flying, which is usually combined with instrument flying, is inherently more dangerous than day flying. If you had engine failure at night and had enough altitude, you bailed out. Another reason it's more dangerous is because a pilot can experience vertigo without realizing it. One night, while taking off in a *SNB* with two students and reaching 300 feet altitude, I saw what I thought was a *Hellcat,* with its very large red and green wing tip lights descending toward me. I thought the pilot was making an emergency landing downwind. My first reaction was to point the nose of my plane down to avoid the fighter. Instead, I checked my gyro horizon instrument; I already was in a nose-down turn. As soon as I leveled my wings and pulled the nose of the plane up to level flight, I saw that those red and green lights were the navigation lights on a drawbridge over the Indian River. I had experienced vertigo.

Another problem became apparent during night-formation flights. Pilots flying wing positions maintained their position by observing a small white light on the top of the fuselage a couple feet behind the cockpit. There were instances when the single light caused a type of fixation similar to being hypnotized. A pilot flying wing position would roll down out of the formation and continue down until he crashed into the water. The solution to the problem was to mount two lights.

For night-strafing over water, two float lights were dropped which helped prevent vertigo. The ocean is completely black under an overcast sky without starlight or moonlight. If your eyes were night adapted on a clear night with only stars, you could easily get a visual view of a blacked-out bogie plane from quiet a distance. The entire bogie and night fighter aircraft were equipped with exhaust dampeners to filter out sparks. Sparks from the exhaust could give away the position of the bogie or the position of a fighter to a bogie gunner.

The low-altitude intercepts at 300 feet, which were practiced over the water five miles east of Vero Beach, were dangerous to fly. The night-fighter pilot, directed by ground-based radar, would get close enough to the target to "lock on" the bogie with radar. The pilot had to constantly scan his flight instruments and radarscope while making small changes in direction and altitude. You only made changes of altitude with your wings level and slight turns only in level flight.

Making a small coordinated turn with a change of altitude was too dangerous. One of my students, Ensign Carney, flew into the water at about 160 knots and only suffered a small gash on his forehead. He was able to get into his life raft and was rescued the next morning. Then he insisted on flying again that night.

We also practiced a skip-bombing technique using a reflective-radar target at the end of a small lake. The fighter's radar would pick up the target as a small blip. With the plane flying at 300 feet at 160 knots, the practice bomb was released at a range of 1,000 feet from the target. The radarscope had a 1,000-foot range marker we made with a black grease pencil on the radarscope.

Night fighter pilots - standing left to right:
first LT Fisher third Ensign Carney - U.S. Navy photo

The radio altimeter was very essential for this bombing run. It had a needle indicator for altitudes from 500 feet to the surface. In addition, there were three, small, colored, warning lights in the cockpit and under the belly of the plane. The green light came on at 500 feet, changed to amber as the altitude approached 400 feet and turned red at 300 feet. On one of my practice bombing runs as I approached the drop point, I caught the reflection of my red-belly light on the water. As I started to pull up, the radio-altimeter needle registered 100 feet! That was too close.

There have been numerous stories written about the *Bermuda Triangle* and the loss of some Navy torpedo bombers flying a navigation training flight from the naval air station at Fort Lauderdale, Florida. Those planes were lost because of a frontal system with unpredictable high winds. The wind blew the torpedo planes well beyond their planned navigational plot to the east. The planes, then, had to buck the high head winds on their return path to Fort Lauderdale; consequently, the pilots would run out of fuel forcing them to ditch their aircraft in very heavy seas. Even if the pilots were able to get in their life rafts, the rafts would have capsized, and the pilots would have drowned.

That night while being directed by RATC, I was flying a night fighter and had climbed up through a solid layer of clouds to get on top of them at 10,000 feet. The winds were so strong that ground control had to keep vectoring me to the west in order to keep my plane over the Vero Beach coastal area.

The most demanding duty officer assignment I ever had in my naval career was supervising the night-flight operations at Vero Beach. The duty assignments lasted two months. The duty schedules were from 1800 until midnight and the next night from midnight until 0400. Three flight instructors rotated the duties. For starters, you monitored a six-page flight schedule for the night fighters and utility bogie flights. The flight schedules had to be continually updated, and the revisions had to be coordinated with RATC, the control tower, flight line personnel, and the pilots in the ready room. Every night there was an average of sixty planes in the air with almost continuous takeoffs and landings. On most nights, the duty was routine, but a bad crash on the runways could make the duty a nightmare.

One night, I had the duty from midnight until morning when we had a congressional investigating group visiting Vero Beach. They were interested in the pilot fatality rates at the Florida air stations. Things started jumping about 0200 when the crash horn sounded, and a flight controller in the control tower yelled over the intercom: "A fighter with a belly tank has just landed wheels up on the main runway, and the plane is on fire." Peeking through a window shutter from my office, I saw the plane was engulfed in fire, and it appeared the pilot was still in the cockpit. The crash truck had not reached the scene. It was a terrifying feeling knowing the pilot was being burned to death in the cockpit.

As I started to leave the office to run up to the control tower, I was met by a trembling, chalk-white-faced pilot who could hardly talk. Then I realized he was the pilot who had just crashed. Miraculously, he was able to escape from the cockpit, running down a wing and clearing the fire. He was one lucky pilot.

The main duty runway had to be closed because of damage from the fire and the debris. A flight instructor, flying a *SNB* was cleared to land on an alternate runway. Being distracted by the confusion and excitement concerning the crash, he landed his plane with its wheels up at the intersection of the other two available runways. Now, all the runways were blocked. Aircraft that had finished their training missions were circling the field with thirty more planes due to land in the hour. After removing the plane from the intersection, we were still landing planes until daybreak. Two fighters had to land just before dawn at an unlighted auxiliary field. Thinking about the congressmen, I joined them for breakfast to tell them about the wild night. Fortunately, no one was killed or injured in the night's fiasco.

Three hurricanes hit the Florida peninsula during 1944-1945. All the flyable aircraft from the Florida air stations had to be evacuated to Georgia and South Carolina. The hurricane weather reporting system was not as sophisticated as today; consequently, there was little time between early warnings and the decisions to evacuate. The air stations didn't want to disrupt flight training prematurely before the storm hit. After the decision to evacuate the aircraft, we had to use all the instructors and some of the flight students to fly the planes out.

On the first evacuation, I didn't even have time to go home for a toothbrush. The fighter planes didn't have baggage compartments, so we didn't carry changes of clothing. On that flight, I was the flight leader for the fighters and ordered to fly to a small military air base at Spartanburg, S.C. The weather was clear until about 100 miles from the air base when we began running into low stratus cloud layers. Finally, we had to descend to get under a solid overcast. The cloud ceilings kept getting lower until we were forced to fly under 500 feet. My greatest concern was the weather at Spartanburg. We were too far away to get radio contact with the control tower to get weather information from the air base, and our planes were getting low on fuel.

It was decision time as to whether to continue on or turn the flight

172

around and try to find an alternate airfield. If the cloud ceiling at the air base was at least 300 feet, we would have enough air space to break the formation and set up an orderly landing pattern. We finally arrived over the field, and I, now, had good radio communication with the control tower. At this time, some of the planes were getting critically low on fuel, and individual pilots started calling the control tower for priority to land. Swamped with calls, the poor control operator could not control the situation which had deteriorated down to a mad scramble to land. Being a flight leader, my aircraft's engine had not burned as much fuel as the other planes. Pilots flying in formation constantly needed to adjust their throttles to hold flight positions and consequently burned more fuel. Therefore, I held off trying to land and could only watch the melee. As I flew around with the few planes still in formation, individual planes with their fuel tanks almost empty dropped out of the formation and headed directly for the runway. All I could do now was watch the fiasco. There was a string of planes with very close intervals rolling down the runway. After all thirty planes were on the ground, the pilots all knew they had lucked out. Nobody had crashed, collided or been killed.

With the second hurricane, the aircraft from Miami and Fort Lauderdale had evacuated late and were landing at Vero Beach. There were two, large flight formations circling above the air station. They were circling in overlapping flight patterns, with each formation passing through solid and broken layers of clouds. If those two formations had collided over the station, we would have had a horrendous situation - multiple mid-air collisions, planes, engines and bodies dropping from the sky. Frankly, I wondered where I should take shelter!

During the last evacuation from Vero Beach, the planes took off in a heavy rain and under a low-cloud ceiling. We flew directly to the coastline at 300 feet and then followed the shoreline north. The weather was clear when we reached Daytona Beach, and we flew on to the Army air base at Macon, Georgia.

That evening, I joined a couple other pilots for a beer in the *Rathskeller* in the basement level of the *Dempsey Hotel*. We observed an amazing sight. Small groups of single women were streaming into the *Rathskeller,* all eyeing the Navy pilots seated at the tables, initiating conversations and sitting down in the empty chairs at their tables. The military draft had cleaned out the young males from the surrounding communities. When our Navy planes flew over Macon and circled the air base, it alerted a lot of lonely girls. Some "fly boys" had arrived.

At 0400 the next morning, an Army sergeant picked up the lower end of my bunk, dropped it to wake me up and said, "Lieutenant, you have orders to evacuate your aircraft immediately to Cortland, Alabama." The first thing I did was call the Dempsey hotel and ask the room clerk to wake up every Navy person registered and tell them they were flying to Cortland, Alabama. Then I routed other pilots out of the Army barracks. Next, I waited for the pilots to arrive at the flight line of our parked planes. A few pilots needed a little remedial attention before I was going to let them fly. Having them run a couple laps around the perimeter of a hanger solved that problem.

While the plane's engines were revving up, I positioned my plane so I could count the planes as they took off. As the planes rolled down the runway and had enough air speed to become airborne, some of the pilots held their planes level with the runway. Then with the wheels still rolling on the runway, they would retract their wheels. They were showing off for the Army boys. If a plane had settled slightly, there would have been a "wheels-up" plane sliding down the runway.

Just as I finished counting the planes that had taken off, I looked up just in time to see a utility pilot named Miller along with Plauche, who was his wingman, close friend and dedicated flat hatter, fly right at and level with the control tower. Just at the last second, their formation split with the two planes passing on each side of the tower! How would you like to have been in that control tower? Thankfully, all the planes arrived safely at Cortland, Alabama and finally at Vero beach.

One day at Vero Beach, the station commanding officer received a personal telephone call from the very irate Army Commanding General of the Army base at Tampa, Florida. Two Navy planes had terrorized the base by repeatedly zooming, extremely low, over the building and trees. It was determined Miller and Plauche were the culprits. Miller was not talking much about the incident. However, when I inspected his plane, it had some small tree branches stuck in the bomb bay doors, and there was a big dent in the bottom edge of the engine cowling. Nothing much happened to them. It just passed as a humorous event at the expense of our Army brethren.

The night-fighter operational training could not have been successful without having bogie aircraft for practicing night fighter intercepts. Those young Marine pilots flew the bogie planes night after night with little personal recognition. In record time, they became skilled and accomplished in night flying. Organized into a utility squadron, the pilots developed a tight bond and camaraderie among themselves and gained the respect of the all the flight instructors and flight students.

The following narrative about the utility pilots called the, *"Epitaph of Utility,"* was written by the colorful, flat-hatter, utility pilot Miller, shortly after the war ended and as flight operations gradually terminated at Vero Beach. This narrative, humorous but also tragic, best describes the adventures of those young pilots. The narrative has been edited to clarify some of the events and jargon. It was salvaged from the bulletin board in the Utility Pilot's ready room after the pilots had departed the air station.

Epitaph of Utility

This is my way of saying goodbye to a bunch of mighty swell fellows. It is written to all of the new Utility pilots and is dedicated to the boys who started the organization of the flying bogies. Any mention of the "Old Marines" means the original "Boondockers" — the Second Lt's, who reported here last summer. In a day or so, I will be hitting the trail away from dear old Vero – the only town I know where it's so quiet after 10 p.m., you can hear the bank drawing interest. It's a town full of lovable inhabitants who spend the summer scratching themselves from mosquito bites. But before I do, I'd like to thank a few guys, congratulate some, and cuss the hell out of a few.

HOOKED

Ole "D.R." was the first utility pilot to report aboard, Oster and Sowa were the second and third respectively. Along with Bratton, Cutler, Remmel and Casey Williams, I watched all the boys come in small groups every two weeks until there were 56 of us. We watched Utility change from a group of disorganized kids to a fairly strong and experienced unit of men. That may sound a little funny to a few of you "Gunsiles," but stop laughing long enough to open your eyes, you'll find that we're all approaching the 1,000-hour mark in our flight log books. For a Second Lt that is quite a few hours. Captain Altizer has only 800, he's a Captain, and we all have around 300 hours of night flying, which will always speak well for us. I'm not blowing smoke up anybody's ass, but those 300-hundred hours have helped me conquer the fear of night flying. I don't know about you fellows, but when I first started here, I actually was afraid every time I took off in the dark. I tried not to let anyone know I was afraid, but I was. I don't love it, understand, don't guess there's anyone that loves it — but the fear is gone, and, and that means quite a bit because the balance of this war is going to see more and more of red-ink flying. [Night-flying hours were logged in red ink.]

When we first started, we were flying the Brewster Buccaneers. Tom Fowler was our boss then. Ole Uncle Tom was a pretty good guy and most of us liked him but he had favorites and that's a poor quality of leadership. He did a good job of organizing us, though, and he made the "pirates" in the flight office well aware of it. None of the Hellcats had radar bulbs yet, and some of the student officers at that time were Jesse "Talk a Little Faster" Walker, Captain "You salute me" McCartney, Fisher and less notorious characters. All the Utility Boys had radio Bat numbers instead of Uncle calls. Those Brewster's were a bitch on wheels. On my second take off, I ground looped into a tetrahedron [a lighted device that pointed into the wind] *with a little loss of urine. Cutler came in with no brakes and took out a large number of trees between here and Jacksonville. Remmel was all set to take off one night when a F6F landed on him.*

But the payoff was the night Oster parked a Brewster on the railroad tracks in front of Andy's Tavern. And to this day, the

176

reason that he got out of the plane so fast was that the accident occurred at 11:14 p.m. and the local express was due any minute.

Then, late in August, those three bladders [Curtiss SB2C dive bombers] started to come in And shortly after, the Brewster's had been condemned and were to be flown to Jacksonville for salvage. What a picnic that was. Thirty of them were built for the Dutch Air Corps, but even the Dutchmen didn't want them. And they all had Dutch instruments in them. Bratton took off and couldn't retract his wheels so he called the tower to land, the tower told him, "Nothing doing — you got it in the air, now get it to Jacksonville." It took him over two hours.

Those three bladers gave us a lot of trouble. Garmany had the first major accident, his engine cut out over the air station. In trying to make the nearest runway, he got slow in the groove and couldn't get his wing up. The cartwheel that followed completely demolished the plane, and left "Ole Misery" setting on his fat ass in the middle of the field between runways 3E and 7E.

And so we settled down to a normal life of engine failures, hydraulic leaks, propeller failures, oil-line breaks, flat tires — and every thing else that makes flying interesting. There came a bond between us — like a big family. We all knew each other, shared our troubles, and held a certain kind of respect for the other guy because we knew what he was up against; we never knew what was going to happen next. The Crash Analysis Officer was a busy man.

We had a few fatalities, which tightened the bond that held us together. I never knew Mike Hornet, but we all remember how his wings folded at low altitude. And I remember the day Neuhaus left to take him home. And Joe Luce, who was flying on my wing, when he crashed and burned to death. Little Davidson was next, and we all know how he died. He was a noisy little guy, but I'll never forget the night when Bloomer put him to sleep on a mattress in the head (toilet). Pilots came from far and wide to see that, and we all had a good laugh. We won't forget Gustovony, either. I can't forget the nights when he would be dancing with Lee Callahan and the Club Mac would echo with, "Oh, You Great Big Beautiful Gustovny." Turner was our next casualty and I hoped it was the last. Captain Altizer says it was pilot error, but I'll never forget that tall, lanky Joe without an enemy on the base. I'd like to take a few lines to put in a plug for Hank Heller who is the only one of us in the Caterpillar Club [a factitious club whose members had to qualify by parachuting out of an airplane].

The FDOs have a plug coming too. Some of you will recall Davey Hyatt, who was first and by far the best of all our rear seat playboys. Haron, Whitey Bayne and other notable characters followed him shortly. The king sized clown badges go to Malone, Jackson, Pellow and Whoresting who were good FDO's and a swell bunch of fellows but the most uneager fellows you'll ever meet. Hass was the busybody, an all time important type. He always knew who was going with who, what girls would put out, and where so and so was at nine o'clock last Saturday night, but I didn't like to fly with him because he tried to boss the show from wheel chock to chock. I've always felt that the pilot was in charge until the fighters had rendezvoused. One night, while I was making my landing approach, Hass called, "Citrus, Zebra One turning base, wheels checked." At the same time, I let go of the stick, and asked Hass if he wanted to land the plane too. Perry Pharr is easy for me to remember because he was in the rear seat the night I crashed and my plane burned off runway 3E.

Hank has had his share of tough luck. Hank had his tail chewed off by an F6F on a dark night at 1,500 feet. He has lost two of his best buddies here. He was flying on Turners wing when "Ole Charlie" bit the dust. He hit the side of Andy King's house – to illustrate; Mrs. King was cooking in her kitchen when she suddenly realized there was no longer a wall between her and the front yard. Here's wishing better luck ahead, Hank.

In February, the new four blader Beasts came in, and it wasn't long before we had 60 of them. Utility will never be the same, I guess, with new faces going in and out, but it's left a lot of memories. I'll always remember the map in Doc Bowes room; the searchlight hops over Orlando at 15,000 feet for 4 ½ hours at a time. Many nights, we shook the rafters at the local nightspots with such memorable hymns as Mountain Dew, Throw a Nickel on the Drum and something about a little pig that slowly walked away.

Before my hands get too tired, I'd like to pass the word to all the new guys in Utility, the bogie pilots have built up a fairly high respect around the base. Whenever Jackpot [radio call name of RATC] *wants a weather report, they ask a Boondocker. People walking to and from the base look up and see some Beasts, they know Utility boys are up there. If you listen closely, you may hear them say, "Let's watch this breakup, or pretty good breakup, or pretty good formation." Our own buddies are watching you too." Occasional they may stop to admire your approach, or say, "Here comes Plauche, lets watch him split S to a landing." The old Marines have a reputation for doing a good job, flying close formation, making tight approaches and drinking more liquor than any other dammed outfit on the base.*

I think I could write a book on Utility if I had more time, but this is more like an epitaph for Utility because, with the war over, the night fighter training operation was slowly grinding to its end. I'm sorry, in a way because, I've grown to like everyone of you fellows. You're a swell bunch of good sports. If we don't meet again, I hope you'll always remember me.

Donald Miller
Second Lieutenant, forever.

HOOKED

Club Mac- Pseudo Officers Club

The wartime mayor of Vero Beach was a Scotsman with the nickname of Mac. He must have become wealthy during the war by providing a wonderful service to all us Navy and Marine types. Mac owned two night-club restaurants. Club Mac — a sort of pseudo officers club — was located right on the beach, and the second club called the Big Apple was located on old Highway 1 within the city limits and catered mostly to the Navy enlisted men. Club Mac's bar had it all. Name your booze. You could order *Schendley's Prewar Reserve* label, but the word *"Reserve"* was blanked out. Other assorted poisons such as *Three Feathers* were sometimes available. The only problem with Mac's bar booze was that the bottle labels became a little worn looking. Once I put a small pencil mark on a half filled bottle, and the next time I was at Mac's, the bottle with the pencil mark was almost full. All the different brands tasted the same and probably came out of the same barrel. Frankly, nobody really cared about the refilled bottles; Mac's Club was such a fun place especially for the utility pilots. They could really shake the floors and walls of that club.

The Navy had leased a beach hotel right next to the club to house the enlisted Waves. Fraternization? Those young Navy and Marine pilots probably didn't know what the word meant. If they did, they could have cared less. The hotel had clothes-lines on the roof, and after one hurricane, there was an assortment of the Wave's dainty undergarments scattered up the beach for over a mile. A provocative sight it was as some swayed from the Palmetto bushes.

After the war ended, it took over six months to close the air station. There was one incident I found hard to forget. A Wave enlisted clerk in the flight office was disposing of files. She asked me what she should do with a waste paper basket filled with pilots' flight logbooks. I looked at some of the names on the logbooks and told her, "Those are log books of pilots killed here." Considering all the flight training conducted during the war, I believe the number of Navy and Marine pilots killed in flight training was greater than those killed in combat.

Annie and I made a sentimental trip to Vero Beach during 1980. We met with an old friend from 1944 whom I had played golf with at that time. He was now an ex-mayor of Vero Beach and a citrus-grove owner. He was also a senior member of the Vero Beach Country Club and hosted Annie and I to a round of golf. We took him and his wife to dinner. Guess where? We dined at a restaurant on the beach where the old Club Mac had previously been located. Unfortunately, a hurricane had destroyed our old haunt.

CHAPTER 20
INTERLUDE BETWEEN WWII
AND KOREAN WAR

S hortly before the war ended, I accepted an officer's commission in the regular Navy from being a reserve officer, and was promoted to Lieutenant Commander. Then I made the decision to remain in the Navy for at least twenty years. With the war finally over, I was looking forward to my first peacetime duty assignment. To say the least, I was a little shocked to receive orders to the Twelfth Naval District, Adak, Alaska, for further assignment. When I arrived home on thirty days leave and talked to my grandfather, he told me, "You're going to the asshole of creation." He had subscribed to the National Geographic magazine for years and had read their descriptions of Adak.

Most carrier pilots knew very little about Alaska but had heard about the number of *PBY's* lost during the war, flying from the air bases in the Aleutian Islands. Now I was going to learn just how tough the flying conditions were in the Aleutians.

Naval Air Station Kodiak

By the time I reported for duty, the Naval District had moved from Adak to the Kodiak Naval Air Station. While being interviewed by the Naval District staff-assignment officer, he told me he needed to fill aviation flight billets at Attu, Adak and Kodiak. During the interview when he mentioned Attu or Adak, I became nervous and uncomfortable. Nobody in his right mind wanted to spend a two-year tour of duty on one of those desolate barren islands. Finally, the decision was made to assign me as the Air Operations Officer for NAS Kodiak. The next best news was that a highly desirable set of living quarters was designated for the Air Operations Officer. Now, I could make flight arrangements to have Annie and my daughter, Susie, join me. They were impatiently waiting in Seattle to hear from me.

Kodiak Island, compared to the rest of the Aleutians, was called, *The Garden Spot of the Aleutian Islands.* It had greenery, fir trees and other foliage. During the two year tour, I had the chance to see how beautiful Alaska was with its great mountain scenery, glaciers, lakes and wildlife. An added bonus was seeing the huge Kodiak and brown bears. Fishing was superb, especially catching large rainbow trout, which were delicious eating because of the firmness of the meat due to the cold water.

During many flights from Kodiak to Anchorage, I flew over the Kenai Peninsula with its beautiful fall foliage. You would occasionally see a large moose. Flying from Anchorage to Fairbanks you passed through Summit Pass, and there was a panoramic view of Mount McKinley and its twin peaks. Mount McKinley is the highest peak in North America at a height of approximately 20,320 feet. In comparison to the 10,000-foot elevation at Summit Pass, Mount McKinley didn't seem to be all that high from our perspective. Down the lower slopes of the mountain were the many glaciers. Fairbanks was especially interesting in the winter; you could see many single snow tracks from dog sleds converging into one main path to the city. It made me wonder if there were road signs along those paths. Fairbanks was pretty far inland, and the winter temperatures could get as low as 60 degrees below zero. At those low temperatures, the moisture from chimneys and car exhausts caused a phenomenon called "ice fog." The areas surrounding Fairbanks could be perfectly clear while at the same time the city would be covered under a thin layer of ice-fog.

In 1912, Mount Katmai blew its top and covered Kodiak Island with over twelve inches of volcanic ash. The explosion of Katmai was ten times greater than Mount St. Helen, and was also was the largest explosion in world history. The mountain is located southwest of Anchorage near the beginning of the Aleutian chain of islands. You could look down into the interior of the crater which was filled with water from melting snow. There are a couple more snow covered mountains farther west, with open craters and white steam continually curling up from snow melting in the warm interior of the craters.

In the spring, the salmon start their runs up the many streams flowing from lakes into the sea to spawn. This is feast time for the brown bears. They wade into the streams and catch salmon in their paws. While flying a twin-engine amphibian plane very low up one of those streams, I counted twenty-one brown bears. As I flew over the bears, one big fearless one swung at the plane with his huge paw.

With Kodiak being so far north, the sun barely goes down in the mid-summer months. It's practically daylight at midnight. On the other side of the coin during the winter months, it would be almost 1000 before daybreak, four hours later at 1400 in the afternoon, the lights needed to be turned on again in the buildings. The vivid, awesome and spectacular displays of the Aurora Borealis, at those northern latitudes, during the winter months are a phenomenon that cannot be described adequately.

As the air station's Air Operations Officer, I was responsible for directing our air station's crash crews. One noon, the crash horn sounded, and the control tower alerted me that a *DC-3* civilian airliner had just crashed as it was landing. When I reached the crash scene, there sat an airliner with its landing gear collapsed and with the diagonal strut for each gear jammed through each wing. The passengers were standing on the runway close to the two pilots, and threatening them. As the story unfolded, it seemed that the pilot was demonstrating to his copilot how to make a short-landing approach by touching down close to the approach end of the short runway. The final moments of the landing approach were over a river and its embankment. The plane dropped down too soon, and the wheels hit the embankment. Apparently, those savvy Alaskan passengers had even been yelling at the pilot during his landing approach saying that he was too low! The airline only owned three planes, the company had just lost a third of its fleet.

The next "on-field" crash was a Naval Air Transport Service (called

NATS) squadron's four-engine *Douglas R5D* transport. Due to unfavorable wind conditions along with just enough rain to make the surface of the runway slick, the plane had to be diverted to a short auxiliary runway that sloped a few degrees downhill. As the plane was rolling down the runway, the pilot didn't have sufficient braking action to slow the plane as it was running out of runway and going too fast to make the turn at the end of it to enter the taxi strip. The plane went off the end of the runway and over an embankment at the edge of the shore line of the bay, and the nose section of the plane was crushed in shallow water.

When I arrived on the accident scene, the crash crew was trying to get the slightly injured pilot out of the debris. His legs were wrapped around the control-wheel-yoke column with his feet entangled in the rudder-control cables. The tide was coming in, and we had about an hour to free the pilot as he risked drowning to death. The first bolt cutters used wouldn't cut the steel cables and it took time to locate larger bolt cutters. As the edge of the tide was lapping over the pilot's feet, the controls cables were finally severed. By getting a blanket under the pilot's heavy body, he was pulled clear of the wreckage.

The great safety feature of the big *R5Ds* having four engines was demonstrated on a flight, on which I was a passenger, while taking off on a short runway at Kodiak with a full load of fuel and cargo. Shortly after the plane became airborne and had reached 300 feet in altitude, the starboard outboard engine had a piston disintegrate, tearing the interior of the engine apart. The plane commander had to keep maximum power on the other three engines to maintain the plane in level flight. He was only able to make a shallow turn away from mountains looming ahead. The plane was shaking and vibrating. Sitting next to me, the group commander of the patrol-plane squadrons based at Kodiak showed no facial expression and just stared straight ahead. Then looking back at the other passengers to see how they were doing, they were also staring straight ahead. A chief petty officer sitting across from me had chained the collar of his large husky dog to a leg of his seat. The dog's ears were laid flat back on his head. Even the dog was scared. The struggling plane was landed without further incident, and the passengers started to relax. The dog's ears were now sticking straight up.

One seaplane flying incident is still vivid in my mind. A naval officer needed to be transported from a small ship anchored in a narrow inlet on the eastern side of Kodiak back to the air station. Here I am volunteering again flying a twin-engine *Grumman JRF* amphibian. I flew over to the inlet and decided that the sea conditions were smooth enough to land, but I noticed there were some small sea swells. This was going to be my first time to land in an almost open-sea condition. The landing was a little rough with the plane bouncing off of the crest of each swell as the plane slowed down and settled in the water. A small boat from the ship transported the officer to our plane.

As I was getting ready for takeoff, the swells looked larger and more ominous than they did from the air. After taxing the plane farther into the inlet where the swells were smaller, I turned into the wind to take off. In a seaplane, you pull the wheel on the control column as far back as it can go and at the same time apply full-engine power. The water spray, from the propellers covers your windshield, obscuring your visibility, until the hull of the plane begins to rise out of the water. As the plane accelerated and hit the first swell, the nose came up. As I pushed forward on the flight controls to ease the nose slightly down, the plane was already on the backside of the swell. You can get into a situation of over controlling, pulling back on the controls, when you need to be pushing forward. Your control actions can get out of synchronization with the movements of the swells. After aborting the takeoff, I then taxied further up into inlet where the swells were smaller. This time before becoming airborne, the hull of the plane was bouncing hard off the tops of swells hard enough that rivets in the hull could have popped out and caused the hull to leak. Again, I had to abort the takeoff. We actually carried common, wooden, lead pencils to plug a hole if a rivet popped out during a takeoff and you needed to land in the water. There was about a half hour of daylight left to get in the air. So, again, I taxied as far up the inlet as possible where the swells were smaller. I told my co-pilot, "I'm not aborting this takeoff again. When our airspeed reaches 40 knots, give me full-down flaps." With the extra lift from the flaps, the plane lightly bounced off the tops of the swells and we were in the air. As I started a right turn away from the mountains, ringing part of the inlet, the right engine's tachometer started unwinding. Thinking the engine was malfunctioning, I braced my foot on the left rudder pedal expecting the plane to swerve hard to the right. There was no engine failure, just a malfunctioning tachometer!

Taking off in that seaplane took all the flight experience I had – wishing I had even more. One thing I learned flying seaplanes, landing in the water in a seaplane is a lot easier than ditching a carrier plane. At least you stay dry! One of the more interesting things about flying seaplanes is the double duty aspect: a sailor on the water and an airman in the air.

On my first flight, as a copilot in the air station's Douglas *R4D* transport plane, we were flying from Kodiak to Dutch Harbor at about 10,000 feet, flying through broken layers of clouds. The moisture in the clouds turned to ice on contact with the propeller blades, leading edges of the wings, and tail surfaces of the plane. Due to my inexperience, I was not aware the plane was picking up some ice. The pilot decided I needed a little education about deicing our propellers. He distracted my attention while he turned on the electrical switch that would start alcohol running from the propeller-hub area out on the surfaces of the blades. In the *R4D,* you can see the engine cowling and the propellers from behind your seat position. There was a loud sharp bang, as something hit the side of the plane just behind my seat. For a second, I was scared, and then I heard the pilot laughing. The noise was due to a piece of ice flying off the propeller and hitting the plane.

As we were letting down to land at Dutch Harbor, I kept looking for the field and a runway. The pilot just kept letting down and looking straight ahead. He was setting me up. Now I'm really getting confused, all I could see were some white buildings ahead of us and couldn't see an air field or a runway. The pilot gave me thumbs down, signaling me to lower our landing gear. Suddenly, he started a sharp 90-degree turn around the edge of the mountain on our right. There was the landing strip, which had been carved out of the base of the mountain next to the edge of the bay.

Take offs had to be made in the same direction, as you land. After taking off you needed to make a full 90-degree turn to clear mountains looming straight ahead. Then, you fly up the valley between two small mountains ranges. Airfields have wind socks to indicate the wind direction. The wind sock at Dutch Harbor, some times, pointed straight up. How could that be? Because the wind off the bay curled up the side of the mountain. Under those wind conditions the airfield had to be closed for flight operations.

The NATS provided regularly scheduled daily logistic and passenger service between Seattle, Kodiak, Adak and Attu. Their planes flew directly from Sand Point Naval Air Station near Seattle to Kodiak going over the Gulf of Alaska. The flights were seldom cancelled due to weather conditions, but some flights had to abort and return to Seattle when they encountered unexpected strong headwinds. They used a navigational checkpoint, a radio-range leg extending out from Vancouver Island into the Gulf of Alaska. When crossing the range leg, the plane commanders had to make a decision about whether they had sufficient fuel to continue on to Kodiak? The lapsed flying time to reach the check point let the pilot estimate the amount of headwinds he was encountering. The weather and wind predictions were usually fairly accurate, so most flights continued to Kodiak.

During the Christmas holidays, military dependent children in schools and colleges in the States could be flown by NATS to Kodiak, Adak and Attu. On one flight with several dependents aboard, a co-pilot, who had just recently qualified as a plane commander, was making his first flight to Kodiak as a plane commander. Most of the flight times averaged about eight hours. He encountered higher winds than expected but made a critical wrong decision to continue on to Kodiak. As the plane approached over ten hours in flight, it was in serious trouble of running out of fuel. There were no search and rescue means available to help if this plane went down in the very cold waters of the Alaskan Gulf. No one would survive.

Two Navy captains with dependents on that plane had joined me along with the officer-in-charge of the NATS detachment in Kodiak in the flight control tower. The radio communications between the plane commander and our control tower were terse. The plane commander sounded very nervous. When the plane was about one hundred miles from Kodiak, it was determined the plane would just barely make it if the estimated distance was correct and with the reported amount of fuel. As I looked into the faces of those two captains, their expressions were grim, and they were visibly frightened. We were on the verge of a terrible tragedy if the plane went down. Finally, we could see the plane's landing lights break through the overcast as the plane was approaching to land. It finally touched down on the runway after being in the air almost twelve hours. The plane only had enough fuel left for about fifteen more minutes of flight.

My two-year Alaskan tour was ending. Flying seaplanes was one of the highlights of my tour. Now I possessed a FAA pilot's license certifying that I was qualified to fly single-engine and multiple-engine land or sea planes. Not many pilots had all those qualifications. Also, although I was an experienced tailhook pilot, I had yet to fly a jet aircraft.

The local Alaskans had an expression when they departed Alaska permanently or on vacations — "We're coming out." Annie was coming out two months before our tour ended. She was pregnant, and because of flight restrictions, she had to fly out before her seven month of pregnancy.

The morning she was to leave Kodiak, there was freezing rain. Two NATS planes were scheduled to depart in tandem. Annie was aboard the second plane, and I was worried. I was concerned about the weather and how quickly the planes could clear the freezing rain as they climbed out. I was in the control tower listening to the radio communications between the first plane and the tower when the pilot reported he had topped the weather layer at 1,500 feet. Thankfully, worries about the safety of my family during the plane's takeoff were over. The tailwinds that day were so strong that it took Annie only four and a half hours to reach Seattle. That set a NATS record for the shortest flight between Kodiak and Seattle.

The officers still wore uniforms at social events, but most of the wives had little choice but to wear the clothes from the same wardrobes they had when they arrived in Kodiak. There were no women's dress shops in the town of Kodiak to replenish their dated dresses. The admiral's wife wore her, one and only, best party gown for two years to all the social functions. Of course, when a new officer's wife arrived on the scene with a little more up to date styled dress it created considerable envy among the wives. Poor Annie, when she arrived back in Seattle wearing her out-of-date short dress and entered a large department store, she said she felt like a country bumpkin. All the other shoppers were wearing ankle-length garments. She told me she started walking with her knees bent so her dress wouldn't look so short.

Naval General Line School
Monterey, California

In 1948, at the end of the Alaskan tour, I received orders to the Navy General Line School at Monterey, California. At the school, the Naval Aviation officer students were taught the rudiments to qualify as general line and ship's officers. These qualifications were necessary in order to advance in your career. The Navy had leased the old Del Monte Hotel in Monterey for the school, and I was in the first class of about 400 students. The classes were over by 1500 and I had the chance to play some golf. It's hard to believe now, but the Monterey Peninsula Country Club let the naval officers become family club members for only twelve dollars a month with all the club privileges except voting! In addition, I had the opportunity to play a round of golf at the famous Pebble Beach course.

Duty in the Navy Department - Bureau of Ordinance
Washington D.C

After finishing the school's final semester, I received orders to the old technical Bureau of Naval Ordnance in Washington D.C. and was assigned to the Procurement Section of the Aviation Ordnance Branch. The section was responsible for administration of the prime contract and 21 subcontracts for a new Navy bombsight being developed.

Most of the contractors were located in the state of New York, New York City and Philadelphia. On one visit to a factory in Philadelphia, I was given a tour of an assembly line for electronic components, with all female workers. I'm wearing my uniform, and many of the gals started whistling at me. What should I do? After grinning back at them, I gave them my best snappy military salute. Then the gals really gave it to me, whistling even louder as I continued down the assembly line.

After two years of Washington duty, I craved the excitement of actively flying in a squadron again. Annie and I were living in the Park Fairfax apartments in Alexandria, Virginia. One of our neighbors was the senior Naval Aviator Duty Assignment Officer in the Pentagon, and he was my "ticket" out of Washington. He approved assignment orders for me to be the commanding officer of a carrier jet squadron based at Naval Air Station Jacksonville, Florida.

When I attended the school in Monterey, California, I had been one of the last of the students to check into the school. I was delayed in reporting because we were expecting our second child. We had been living with my mother in Wisconsin until Annie delivered our little bundle of joy, Bobbie, in late January 1948. By the time we arrived in Monterey, all available rental housing was taken, so we had to buy a home in Carmel. When I finished school, we put our house on the market. We received an offer to buy our home, accepted it and then departed for Washington D.C. After arriving in Washington, we were informed by our real estate agent that the buyer had backed out of the deal. The agent rented the property but the amount of rent, due to rent control in that area, was insufficient to cover our mortgage loan payments and expenses. The property had become a financial liability and, in addition to that, also had some associated property management problems. I wanted to get back to the west coast to get our house sold, so I asked my good neighbor, the aviation detail officer, to change my orders to a Pacific Fleet squadron. That was a major mistake. The new orders directed me to report to the Commander of the Pacific Fleet in San Diego for further assignment.

At this point in time, it looked like the Korean War was about over. General MacArthur's armies had pushed to the Yalu River. When the North Koreans had attacked South Korea, carrier aircraft flying off the *USS Valley Forge* were in the news. What caught my attention while I was watching the news on TV was that the aircraft were *Navy Corsair* fighters. Little did I know I would end up flying 80 combat missions over North Korea in the *Corsair.*

CHAPTER 21
FIGHTER SQUADRON FIFTY THREE

After the movers packed all our family's worldly belongings, Annie, our two daughters and I embarked on a cross-country trip to San Diego in December of 1950. As we were driving through Elko, Nevada, on a cold blustery day with snow flurries, we were listening to the radio and heard a flash news announcement. Chinese armies had crossed the Yalu River and were attacking in strength. All the previous news about the war had been good. After our troops had pushed all the way to the Yalu River, there was talk that the war would soon be over, and some of our troops could be coming home for Christmas. With the Chinese armies entering North Korea in strength, it was the beginning of a new bloody and brutal phase of the war.

My first reaction was disbelief. After looking into Annie's face I could see she was shocked. At first, we both were lost in our own thoughts. Our daughters were asleep in the back seat of our car, and they were too young to have understood what the impact of the terrible news had on us. After gathering my thoughts, I told Annie, "I have volunteered myself into another war." Then, questioning myself, "Why did I give up a cushy job in Washington?" Annie was going to sweat it out again for a year most likely while I flew combat missions off a carrier. Why hadn't I thought more about Annie and my two daughters when I decided I wanted to leave Washington? Annie had already experienced too many hectic times during our marriage to now have to worry about me flying combat missions again.

The headquarters for the Commander Air Forces Pacific Fleet ("ComAirPac") was located at NAS North Island, just across San Diego Bay and adjacent to the City of Coronado. After reporting to the assignment officer in the Personnel Division of ComAirPac, I received orders as the executive officer of Fighting Squadron Fifty Three. The squadron was assigned to Air Group Five, to be deploying aboard the *USS. Essex*. The *Essex* would be conducting combat operations in support of the United Nation's peacekeeping mission in Korea. The squadron would be flying the famous *Corsair F4U-4Bs* fighter, a WWII vintage propeller aircraft. What a let down, I had turned down the chance to be the commanding officer of a jet fighter squadron.

Annie wanted to live in Coronado, so we checked into a motel there, so we could start hunting for a rental apartment or a residential home. Christmas was upon us before we found suitable lodging, and spending the holiday in a motel room with a sparsely decorated Christmas tree was particularly tough on my daughters.

On Christmas Day, all the restaurants in Coronado were closed except the Mexican Village restaurant, which the Navy pilots called "MexPac." The bar area was jammed with young, single naval aviators trying to get into the Christmas spirit. We had to weave our way through the partying pilots to get to the dining room. Eating Mexican food on Christmas Day, instead of the traditional holiday fare was truly a novelty, but for us this was the most dismal Christmas our family ever spent together.

Squadron Flight Training

On the 28 December 1950, I made my first flight in a squadron *Corsair F4U-4B* at North Island Air Station. The wind was from the east, and the takeoffs took you directly over barracks and office buildings leaving no place to go if your engine quit at that time. Our squadron flight training was intense and thorough. The squadron deployed twice for two weeks to the naval air station at El Centro, CA, where we practiced firing rockets, strafing, glide bombing and FCLP.

Getting carrier qualified once again was going to be quite an undertaking due to a problem I wasn't expecting. The *Essex* operated a few miles off the west coast from San Diego to conduct carrier qualification landings. During landing operations, the *Essex's* speed would be about 28 knots with an average wind of 15 knots. The wind across the flight deck would be close to 40 knots. Jet aircraft required more wind across the deck than the propeller aircraft. Carrier landings now were quite different than landing on the old *Hornet* in 1942 where the *Hornet* struggled to do 25 knots.

In modern jet carrier operations, the jets fly a straight-in approach, flying down a predetermined glide path to an angled flight deck. During the Korean War era, the propeller and the early-version jet planes used the old system called "constant-speed, constant-altitude" for carrier landings. As your aircraft is flying downwind, you sight a line reaching from the top of the carrier's island structure to the opposite horizon line. Being on that line, the aircraft is at the ideal altitude of about 300 feet. The decision of when to break into your 180-degree turn toward the ship is a critical judgment call. The variables are the ship's speed and the wind velocity.

My first attempted landing almost killed me. Looking at the *Essex,* I started downwind and then realized if I commenced the 180-degree turn as I was opposite the ship's bow position — as I did on the slower *Hornet* — I would be too far downwind when I finished the final part of the turn. We called that situation being "sucked behind." I started my 180-degree turn at about a half ship's length ahead of the *Essex's* bow, and as I progressed into the turn, I got sucked behind. I aborted and then flew ahead of the ship to set up for another approach to land. This time, I turned almost two ship lengths ahead of the bow position. As I was completing the turn and was picked up by the LSO, he was giving me a roger. I'm approaching what I thought was a perfect position for a cut signal to land. Now the trouble started. The LSO should be giving me the cut signal. Now, I'm looking down at the LSO at about a 70-degree angle; he hadn't given me the cut. My mind said "cut," and I took my own cut. The deck felt like it was running away from me. My tailhook snagged the first arresting wire, the wire closest to the stern ramp. If I had taken the cut a full second earlier, my plane could have crashed into the ramp. Having been a LSO, I knew I had committed the cardinal sin of taking my own cut. With the high wind across the deck, you had to be looking almost straight down at the LSO and just over the front edge of your left wing when the LSO gave the cut signal.

After being directed up the flight deck to be parked, I headed for our ready room to meet the LSO. He was glaring at me and wanted to know what possessed me to take my own cut? All I could say was, "I'm just an old dog trying to learn a new trick." The next day on my first landing, I took my hand off the throttle lever as I approached the LSO waiting for the cut. This old dog's plane caught the third wire; I had mastered my new trick.

As our training program progressed, the commanding officer of the squadron asked me to work individually with a squadron pilot having trouble flying the *Corsair*. After having him fly on my wing position for a few flights, he seemed to lack confidence in his own ability while flying certain maneuvers and was afraid of getting into a spin. The *Corsair* was not restricted from doing spins, but the Pilot's Handbook didn't recommend doing them.

After reviewing spin recovery techniques with the pilot, I decided to have him watch me demonstrate a spin in the Corsair. I climbed up to 10,000 feet over an unpopulated area. Then I pulled the plane up to a vertical position until the air speed dropped off to 40 knots. I cut the throttle. This put the plane into a "Hammerhead stall." The plane was almost falling down backwards, the nose dropped violently, the plane leveled out almost horizontal as it entered a vicious flat spin. The rudder pedals were jerking against my feet. The control stick was beating back and forth between my knees, and the plane was rapidly losing altitude. I pushed the control stick as far forward as I could get it, trying to get the nose of the plane to drop to an almost horizontal position. As I watched my altitude drop down below 4,000 feet, I was thinking of bailing out. Still trying to get the nose to drop, in desperation, I pulled back hard on the throttle getting it completely off. The nose of the plane suddenly dropped down, the plane stopped spinning as the airspeed increased, and then I was able to level the plane at 2,500 feet. After landing at North Island and walking back to the hanger, I asked the other pilot what he thought about the spin. He said, "You scared the hell out of me." I wasn't about to tell him I had almost bailed out.

On 23 June while driving from home to the squadron office, I noticed the *Essex* tied up at the dock instead of being at sea conducting scheduled carrier qualifications. Feeling apprehensive as I entered our squadron office, the news wasn't good; our planned deployment date to Yokosuka, Japan, had changed. The air group had four days to get our planes and equipment aboard the *Essex*. The *Essex* and the air group received orders to proceed to Hawaii, to be on a standby basis for six weeks, and then deploy to Yokosuka.

This last-minute schedule change was demoralizing for our families. This is where the Navy wives and families were tested. During this war, most of the pilots were married and had small children, and the majority of the pilots were reserve pilots called back to active duty. Some pilots would lose new businesses they had started after WWII.

In checking, I found out that most of the younger pilots only had the standard, government, life-insurance policies for $10,000. Only one insurance company that I could find would write a $10,000 term policy without a war clause. After arranging a meeting with an agent and our squadron pilots, I tried to convince the pilots that this was their last chance to get additional coverage, reminding them that we were going into a shooting war. None of the pilots signed up for more insurance. Unfortunately, we lost three of our squadron pilots in combat over North Korea.

The afternoon the *Essex* was preparing to leave the dock at North Island, a somber group of squadron pilots and their families congregated on the dock waiting for the deadline before reporting aboard. One of our squadron pilots reporting for his second Korean combat tour gazed up at the planes on the flight deck and quietly told me, "There's going to be some of us that might not make it back." Seventeen of the air group pilots were not going to make it back.

The first few days at sea takes a little adjustment, getting used to being away from your families and the barren feeling of the ship. As the *Essex* neared Pearl Harbor, the air group aircraft flew to Barbers Point Air Station located near Pearl Harbor. For the next six weeks, we usually flew practice-bombing flights in the mornings, relaxed on the beach in the afternoons and then in the evenings lounged around in the officers club. Things were too easy. I was becoming apprehensive about the future thinking, about the winter combat missions that lay ahead.

CDR Fisher, squadron executive officer VF-53 – 1951

CHAPTER 22
KOREAN WAR

Combat Flight Operations

On 25 August, the *Essex* accompanied by another carrier joined a task force operating in the Sea of Japan. Our air group would conduct combat operations for thirty days on the "line" — the combat zone — and then return to Yokosuka for two weeks for rest and recreation (R & R) along with the ship's crew and air group personnel. During the seven-month tour, the Essex would deploy four times, each with thirty days on the line. The *Essex's* planned combat tour would be over on 24 February 1952 at the end of the fourth 30-day period. Due to a mishap that delayed the carrier assigned to relieve the Essex on station, we all had to stay on the line an additional ten days. Our squadron lost another — and our last — pilot during that ten-day period.

Combat operations commenced on 26 August 1951, and our squadron lost our first pilot on that day. He was flying in a formation that penetrated an overcast layer of clouds, and when the flight climbed up and cleared the clouds, he never reappeared. After an intense search, the wreckage of his plane was never sighted. That same day, I flew my first combat mission over North Korea. This was very different from my combat experience flying in WWII where you were flying mostly over the ocean. Here you were flying over land on all combat missions – you're flying over enemy territory. If you were shot down and survived, you were doomed to become a POW unless you were picked up by rescue helicopters, which we called "Helos." My greatest fear was not being killed but becoming a POW and being tortured. Also, it was rumored that POWs would never be repatriated. In fact, some of the *F-86* jet fighter pilots shot down over North Korea were turned over to the Russians – supposedly for interrogation reasons – and their fates have never been revealed.

Carrier flight operations during the winter months made brutal working conditions on the flight deck. When the flight deck and planes were covered with snow and ice, sometimes it was necessary to move the task force south to warmer weather to melt the ice. The sea temperatures in Wonsan Bay were very cold, approaching 33 degrees in January.

Clearing snow off USS Essex flight deck - January 1952 - U.S. Navy photo

In October, pilots were issued a new type of survival suit, nicknamed "poopy suits," in which a pilot could survive for about two hours in the icy waters of the Sea of Japan. Underneath the suits, we wore long-handle underwear, a special padded undergarment, and two pairs of ski socks. You climbed into the green, nylon, rubber-impregnated survival suit through a slit in the torso area, first pushing your feet and legs into the bottoms that were form fitted. Then you pushed your arms through the sleeves which had black latex-rubber openings that sealed tightly around your wrists. We then pushed our heads into the latex-rubber neck section. The final step when donning the poopy suit was to roll up the lengthy material on each side of the opening, which had been folded down just like a paper sack. The slit opening was now sealed closed and finally fastened shut with snaps. To protect our hands, we wore surgical rubber gloves, covered by thin nylon ones to protect the rubber gloves, and finally winter flight gloves. For our feet, we wore Marine-issue, winter, rubber field shoes.

Supposedly, your feet would not freeze even if your socks were wet. Over the top of the survival suit, we wore the standard, inflatable, aviation life jacket. Because we were flying over land, we needed a land-survival jacket, which we improvised from Army jungle-survival vests. We wore this jacket over the life jacket. There was nothing standard about the items each pilot included in his jacket. We all carried a loaded 38-caliber pistol, extra ammo, a small flat can of water, cans of dehydrated food, morphine syringes and ozone tablets to purify drinking water. We were told the water in Korea was contaminated even near mountain tops. Before takeoffs, I unbuttoned my jungle-survival vest, so I could shed it quickly if I ever had to ditch. We were so top heavy wearing the bulky paraphernalia, we could potentially end up floating in a head-down position in the water. Our plane captains had to give the pilots a "leg-up" lift to a wing, so we could climb into the cockpits.

You don't realize how much protection the poopy suits gave a pilot until it's your life that's on the line. A reminder of that surfaced once when I ripped open the right sleeve of my suit accidentally. One of our pilots had been hit, and I thought he might be in trouble. I hurriedly reached down along the side of the cockpit to grab a map, so I could pinpoint the pilot's location in the event he had to bail out or crashed. My sleeve caught on something sharp, and there went my water-tight integrity.

Thankfully, the emergency situation was over, and there was only one thought in my mind, "Get back to the Essex as soon as possible." If my engine quit, and I was forced to ditch, I could only survive a few minutes in the cold water because of the rip in my survival suit. The *Essex* was about sixty miles away, and it seemed like I flew a hundred miles until I was circling the ship to land.

Squadron pilot LTJG Prichard modeling "poopy suit" - U.S. Navy photo

Our Corsair's carried a 1,000-pound bomb or a napalm bomb, two 250-pound bombs and a single 100-pound bomb on each wing. On our first flight off the *Essex* after returning from our "R and R," we flew warm-up flights sans the bombs, and we only used 58 inches of manifold pressure for our takeoffs. On the next day after a warm-up flight with a full-ordnance load, I doped off and started down the flight deck using only 58 inches of manifold pressure instead of necessary 62 inches.

Our rescue helicopter always hovered off the starboard bow slightly ahead of the ship's island structure monitoring each plane's takeoff. When I observed the shadow of our helo moving forward because my plane was moving too slow, I knew I was in serious trouble. My manifold pressure was only at 58-inches!

I jammed the throttle hard forward to 62 inches as I was approaching the end of the flight deck. My plane settled as it cleared the bow. I managed to retract my landing gear, and with the air-cushioning effect under my wings and with the water, the plane barely remained airborne. The helo pilot told me my propeller's blast was blowing ripples on the water and mist in the air.

F4U-4B Corsair ready for takeoff on combat mission - U.S. Navy photo

On most of our combat missions, we flew eight *Corsair* fighters and teamed up with eight Douglas *AD* bombers. Those *ADs* carried more bombs than the WWII *B-17* bombers - a 2,000-pound bomb under the belly, 1,000-pound bombs outside the wheels, three 250-pound bombs and two 100-pound bombs under each wing. One *AD* in each flight carried an aerial camera mounted on a wing for taking photographs of the damage and destruction from the bombs.

Douglas AD Bomber with full bomb load on flight deck of Essex
Fisher photo

The *AD* pilots had to make multiple-bombing runs and dropped each large bomb separately, exposing their aircraft to even more AA. The squadron lost seven pilots, and replacement pilots had to be ordered into the squadron.

Tragedy on the flight deck

On 16 September, we had a tragic event on the flight deck of the Essex. A *F2H-2* jet pilot had a slight mid-air collision with another plane damaging his right aileron. He didn't have full control of the plane, making it difficult to safely land. Jet pilots rushed out of their ready room to taxi their planes forward near to the bow of the ship to clear the landing area. As I was circling downwind, I watched the jet pilot approaching on his final leg and touching down on the deck.

For a moment, I thought, "He made it!" Instead, the plane just continued up the flight deck, its tailhook was not down! The plane careened into the jets that had just been taxied forward. Some of the taxi-pilots were trapped in their cockpits when all hell broke loose. First, a small ball of fire erupted, followed by an explosion, and a huge fire. Burning jet fuel from a parked jet's ruptured wing tip-tanks cascaded down the starboard side of the ship.

F2F-2 Banshee jet fighters flying past Essex - U.S. Navy photo

Initial explosion
U.S. Navy photo

Damage control crew fighting fire
U.S. Navy photo

Burning fuel cascading over edge of Essex deck - U.S. Navy photo

One of the parked burning jet planes, with a pilot still in the cockpit, fell off the flight deck into the water. The pilot was rescued but suffered severe facial and ear burns. The out-of-control plane had first run over a chief petty officer, a flight-deck plane director, killing him. The jet pilot died from the impact and fire. Eight sailors also died, either killed in the fire or died later of their severe burns. If the plane had swerved up the forward port side of the flight deck, it would have crashed into *AD* bombers loaded with their large bombs. If some of those bombs had exploded, we could have lost the *Essex.* My flight had to be diverted to a Marine airfield in Korea called King 18. It was dusk as we left the *Essex.* When we reached King 18, it was pitch black, and there were no runway lights. A ground crew was slowly positioning flickering kerosene filled pots along one edge of the, Marston type, steel-matted runway.

The last field landings any of the *Essex* pilots had made were at Barbers Point Air Station last August. After making carrier landings, landing on a runway felt like you were tearing down the runway at hundred knots or better. The plane's tires really sang rolling on the matting. As we taxied our planes off the runway to a dirt taxi strip, the air blasting from our propellers raised a huge cloud of dust, and we had to don our oxygen masks to keep from inhaling the dust. One great advantage of being a carrier pilot was our planes were always clean. A Marine *Corsair* pilot told me they were sometimes lucky to get even one gun to fire because of the guns being contaminated by dirt. Of course, our plane captains hated the sight of our dirty planes when we arrived back aboard ship. It meant a lot of hard work scrubbing those planes down with soap and water.

We were able to return to the *Essex* the next morning. With the debris from the fire removed from the flight deck, normal flight operations were underway. Our ship's medical doctors needed Cortisone to treat the burn victims. Our group commander flew into a Seoul, Korea, air force base, and I flew to another air base to pick up Cortisone. When I picked up the package of Cortisone, the small size of the package surprised me; it was small enough to fit in a pocket of my flight suit. Between the group commander and me, we were carrying half of the Cortisone available in South Korea back to the *Essex.*

KOREAN WAR

Kapsan, North Korea
A Highly Classified Special Target

On 29 October, I led eight *Corsairs* followed by eight *AD* bombers, led by their squadron commander, to attack a special assigned highly classified target located at Kapsan, that was located about fifty miles south of the Manchurian and North Korean border on the eastern side of Korea. Military intelligence had information about an important 0900 meeting at Kapsan of senior Chinese, North Korean VIP military and political leaders. During our pilot's briefing, we knew the Kapsan target was out of range if our plane went down and we needed to be rescued by helos. It was inferred that if your plane went down and before you were captured that you might want to make a choice to either shoot yourself or risk being tortured to death. I had already made up my mind; I wasn't going to be captured alive.

Our flight flew at low altitude until we were about fifty miles from Kapsan and then climbed to 8,000 feet. As I approached Kapsan and started my dive, it was 0900. The target area was well landscaped. There was a tall radio-communication mast and a complex of scattered buildings. We had executed a complete surprise with no sign of AA. On my first bombing run, I selected the largest building nearest the radio mast. Each *AD* pilot made several individual "bombing runs," and while the *ADs* were completing their runs, our *Corsairs* strafed smaller buildings and vehicles. We had been over Kapsan for almost an hour, and I was getting nervous. A jet-fighter attack could be launched from airfields close to the border in Manchuria.

Luckily, none of our planes were hit, and all returned safely to the *Essex*. Later that afternoon, the radios transmitting news from Pyongyang, North Korea went ballistic and called Navy pilots butchers. A U.S. Marine captain operating with North Korean partisans reported a bomb shelter had been penetrated by one of our large bombs and killed over 300 people. Years later, I heard the Marine agent never got out of North Korea, and all the partisans had been hunted down and killed.

Air attack on Kapsan, North Korea - U.S. Navy photo

Air attack on Kapsan, North Korea - AD bomber upper center of photo
U.S. Navy photo

Our squadron's aircraft had a large white identification letter S painted on their rudders and could easily have been identified during those bombing runs at low altitude. After that mission, I hated flying interdiction missions beyond range of the rescue helos because if captured, you knew you'd be tortured and then killed. All the pilots who flew the Kapsan mission were awarded Distinguished Flying Crosses.

The Bridges of Toko Ri

The movie, *Bridges of Toko Ri,* was an entertaining movie, but far from authentic. James A. Michener wrote the book about the bridges, and he coined the name "Toko Ri." The motion picture followed the book of the same title. Michener had come aboard the *Essex* in 1952 to gather material for his planned book. He actually flew on a night-attack mission in an *AD* bomber. Some railroad box cars were bombed that night, and a steel ladder rung from a box car was found imbedded in the belly of the fuselage of the *AD* after the plane landed back aboard the *Essex.*

The bridges were four railroad bridges across a winding river. The rail line that crossed those bridges connected with a rail line on the east coast of Korea and one on the western side of Korea in an area in the narrow waist of Korea. The eastern junction of the railroads was about forty-five miles northwest of Wonsan Bay. The bridges were vital links in the railroad supply lines which supported the North Korean and Chinese armies. They were heavily defended, and some of the AA guns were radar controlled. The guns were located on various, strategic mountain-area positions and could shoot laterally across our dive paths in our bombing runs. Attacking those bridges was tough and very dangerous. We lost Ensign Bateman - "the baby" in our squadron. He was only twenty-two years old. A portion of one of his wings was blown off, and the plane spiraled down to crash into the side of a mountain. When we were operating with two carriers, the carrier's air groups alternated mission assignments of the bridges to spread the risk. Our pilot losses were high because we could not locate the camouflaged gun positions and destroy them, but Mother Nature would have a hand in turning things around.

LTJG Riebeling, Ensign Bateman, CDR Fisher and LTJG Hogan
Personal photo

In late fall, the foliage fell off the trees, and we had the first heavy snow which exposed the enemy gun positions. *F9F Cougar* jets configured with aerial cameras flew at low altitudes and captured detailed pictures of the positions. Those pictures revealed seven major gun positions.

An all-out coordinated air-group attack was launched from the *Essex* with individual gun positions assigned to the pilots. Jet fighters started the attack firing 5-inch rockets, I followed leading eight *Corsairs,* and we dropped 1,000-pound bombs with proximity fuses. Lastly, the *ADs* dropped 1,000 and 2,000-pound bombs also with proximity fuses. We dropped the bombs from 3,000 feet crossing the valley laterally and the bombs exploded in the air above the gun positions. When those bombs exploded, they looked like miniature atomic bombs: a big bright orange flash and then a mushroom cloud of smoke. As we turned around and climbed up to make a second bombing run across the valley, there was no AA.

Now, we could attack the bridges without the murderous AA. Previously, we had been attacking the bridges flying a longitudinal path to the bridges and then dropping the bombs at low altitudes, but, instead, we surprised the enemy by first flying laterally and then dropping our bombs at 3,000 feet.

We didn't have too much trouble with ground-fire when we were "Cutting the rails," which is dropping bombs about every half mile in the rural areas, but near bridges and military populated areas, it was a completely different story. In the area south between Wonsan and the "Bomb-line" (front line) between the opposing armies, there were three enemy armies in place, and it was a very "hot" area to fly over.

A Key Bridge

The executive officer of the *AD* squadron and I "drew" a mission in that area to bomb a concrete highway bridge to destruction, which meant to make additional bombing runs until a bridge span was dropped. The bridge was in a valley with 3,000-foot mountain peaks on each side of the valley and highly defended by 40mm and larger caliber AA guns. The *AD* flight leader and I, both being dive-bomber pilots in WWII, decided this was too dangerous a target area to use our normal glide bombing tactics, so we planned to start our dives from 10,000 feet diving as steeply as possible, almost like dive bombing.

When we arrived at the target area, there was a high layer of clouds right over the valley and target area, which forced us to circle to lose altitude to 7,000 feet. Leading the *Corsairs* ahead of the *AD* bombers, I rolled into a steep dive and immediately watched fiery orange balls leaving trails of smoke from the 40mm stuff missing me off my right wing. A high wind was drifting my plane to the left off the path line to the target.

Fortunately, the last *AD* bomber pilot made a direct hit with a 2,000-pound bomb on the bridge and dropped a span of that bridge. He was the hero of our flight! After pulling out of our dives and trying to clear the area so we could join up in formation, we were encountering extremely heavy AA. I saw the *AD* flight leader make a hard evasive turn with multiple white bursts from AA trailing close behind him. I yelled to warn him, and he yelled back, "You have the same problem."

We had stirred up a hornet's nest, but, luckily, we didn't lose a plane. After we cleared the area, we headed back toward Wonsan. It was about an hour before sunset. And on the way back, we spotted a number of Army trucks moving toward a road from their camouflaged positions. It reminded me of seeing bugs swarming when you lifted up an old wet board. We didn't have any bombs left, so we strafed the trucks. The drivers made no attempt to pull off the road and seemed to ignore us. Our *Corsair* night-fighter pilots told us that every night they would see long lines of trucks with dim headlights traveling down the roads.

Pilot Rescue Operations

During the Korean War, land-based helos would fly to their maximum flight ranges to rescue a pilot. In spite of the extreme danger of those pilot rescue operations, the helo pilots always tried to respond. When one of our squadron pilots was down on the ground, we called for a helo and remained circling the pilot's position at 300 feet firing at anybody trying to approach the pilot. We used grid maps to locate targets and pilots' positions.

Late one afternoon, we tried to get a helo in to rescue a downed pilot from another carrier. He had parachuted into a steep slope above a valley where there was a lot of ground fire from the area below. While I was making a steep diving run into the valley, trying to locate the pilot's position, following close behind me was a continuous string of white AA bursts. It was too hot an area to bring in the helo, and I told the pilot not to continue the rescue attempt. Instead, he flew his helicopter over the mountain ridge, started down the slope, until his radioman was wounded. The pilot then aborted the rescue attempt, but, at least, he had tried. The Koreans captured the downed pilot and released him with other POWs near the end of the hostilities.

The helos had a bad day during a pilot-rescue attempt. Two were hit, and both pilots and their radiomen were killed. On New Year's Day, 1952, while flying on a mission and monitoring our common emergency radio channel, I heard chatter about an Air Force pilot being down. The pilot, spotted on the ground by an observer flying

215

over the scene said, "They're dragging him under a tree and beating him with their rifles." What a way to start the New Year.

There is a small island, called Yodo Island, located on the eastern edge of Wonsan Bay. It was held by our friendly forces and surrounded by mine fields. This was a safe area where pilots could ditch their disabled planes. The commanding officer of our *AD* squadron ditched there five times. In September, the sea-water temperature had lowered, and it became necessary for the pilots to wear survival suits. We had not yet received new type survival suits that were more efficient. The first survival suits we had were nothing but a rubber suit with a drawstring to tighten the suit around your neck, and they would fill up with water. In addition, the suits were hot to wear, and you could become dehydrated while flying. After a three-hour flight, you would drain the accumulated water from the suit onto the ready room deck.

The following rescue operations happened before the new type survival suits were available in October. Two of our pilots almost lost their lives from hypothermia while wearing those suits after parachuting into the cold water.

Our squadron operations officer had his engine hit by AA west of Wonsan. His engine was streaming fire and smoke as he was trying to reach the ditching area near Yodo Island. After using his parachute, he landed in the water near a Navy rescue ship. As the ship came alongside, he struggled to untangle his parachute shroud lines. A sailor from the ship dove into the icy water and saved the pilot's life. The pilot wrote a letter to the sailor thanking him for rescuing him. Here is an excerpt from the letter: *"I was hurt; I was numb with cold and hung up in my parachute. I knew I could not last much longer."*

Another squadron pilot also had to use his parachute and landed in the water near Yodo Island. A helo hoisted him out of the water, but his deflated parachute dragging in the water almost stopped the helo from reaching the rescue ship. His wet flight suit iced up as soon as he was pulled out of the water. He was lucky and only suffered from frost bitten fingers.

KOREAN WAR

Close Air Support Missions

Our close-air support missions supported our ground troops by strafing, dropping conventional bombs and napalm bombs. Dropping napalm bombs was very dangerous. You had to release the bomb at low altitudes flying almost in level flight to make the napalm spread on the target area. It was a terrible weapon when used against ground troops. My first napalm drop was on entrenched Chinese troops. As I pulled up, I could see troops, scrambling in panic, running down a steep slope trying to clear the burning area. Planes following my flight, strafed the area with their 20mm canons firing explosive shells. Those exploding shells from each plane had the same effect as dropping a bushel basket of hand grenades. The napalm-bomb tanks we used were old WWII Japanese aircraft belly tanks recovered from Japanese aircraft storage dumps. The tanks had bomb shackles and a bomb fuse adapter welded to the tanks. Some of those tanks were badly dented, and one tank that was hung on my plane had the nose completely flattened. It was not streamlined, not a thing of beauty, but an economical solution to a shortage of tanks.

One problem with flying close air-support missions against enemy ground troops was the possibility of hitting our own troops when the troops were only yards apart. Army pilots called "mosquitoes" — we called them "spotters" — flew old North American *T-6* basic-training aircraft that had rocket rails installed and could fire smoke rockets to pinpoint our assigned ground targets. When the spotter assured himself that the Navy pilots had visually identified a target, he would give us an okay to hit the target. It took sheer guts to be a spotter pilot, flitting around low over the enemy trying to avoid the pot shots. It was almost like a fly buzzing around avoiding the swatter. Sometimes the swatter scored a hit.

There was a "hot" ground area called the "Punch Bowl" which straddled the front lines. The enemy troops were dug in on the north rim, and our troops were dug in on the south rim. Our troops had positioned orange and red cloth panels to mark their positions. After clearance by a spotter, I led an eight-plane flight down over our own troops while strafing the enemy target. The brass shell casings from our 20mm cannons were dropping in our own troop area. The small-arms fire from the enemy troops was intense. The only good thing about flying close air support was if you had to bail out, you'd had a chance to land in friendly territory.

An interesting thing about all the territory north of the extended bomb-line clear across North Korea was the lack of activity north of the bomb-line. The enemy armies were masters of camouflage in hiding and dispersing their motor vehicles, tanks, ammunition dumps, and especially how they concealed their steam locomotives. During the daytime nothing moved. South of the bomb-line everything could move because we had air control. You could see clouds of dust from moving trucks and artillery firing white phosphorous shells into enemy troop positions.

Deep Interdiction Missions

Most of our missions were interdiction missions deep behind the bomb-lines. Rail trains were vital to supplying the enemy armies. We had to destroy the rail lines by dropping bombs about every mile in a ten-mile section. Navy planes flying interdiction missions had destroyed the major railroad bridges over rivers during the first few months of the war. It was amazing how fast the rail lines and temporary small bridges were repaired. The large bomb craters would have the void filled by using railroad ties to form a bridge. During the winter months after snow covered most of North Korea, I never observed bulldozer tracks. Most of those rail and bridge repairs had been done by hundreds of individuals working under brutal weather conditions.

In order to hit the rail tracks, you had to glide-bomb (shallow dive about 30-40 degrees) at low altitudes, around 300 feet and pull up sharply to avoid your own bomb blast. A few of our planes had dents in their bellies from bomb debris. Most of our pilot losses were from 50-caliber and 20mm guns hitting their planes at low altitudes.

Large bomb hit on rail road track - U.S. Navy photo

Bomb driven into side of railroad bed showing the rails bent 30 degrees
U.S. Navy photo

During the thirty days, the task force operated in the Sea of Japan, the ships in the task force needed refueling periodically. The carrier's air combat operations depleted the bombs and aviation fuel in three days. On the fourth day, an ammunition ship and then an oil tanker steamed parallel with the *Essex*. They transferred bombs using nets and oil through hose lines suspended on heavy lines rigged between the ships. Bombs almost completely covered the *Essex's* hanger deck, and as work crews bolted fins on the bombs, other work crews then took the bombs down elevators to the magazines.

The pilots welcomed getting the day off from flying combat missions. Our pilot attrition rate averaged out to losing one pilot every ten days we flew combat strikes. That mathematical fatality rate started to get into your mind as our combat tour slowly continued. Each pilot normally flew one mission a day except during the longer summer and early fall days when some pilots had to fly two missions. The *Corsair* and *AD* bomber missions averaged over three and a half hours and the jets one and a half hours. Each flight required about an hour of pre-briefing, suiting up in flight gear, and, at the end of the flight, another hour of debriefing.

Occasionally when my flight was returning to the *Essex* after flying a combat mission, I would ask my wingman, John Hogan, to fly ahead of the formation and do a series of eight-point acrobatic slow rolls. It was a very difficult precision maneuver to be able to momentarily pause at each point in the roll. John was a superior pilot, and all the pilots in the flight gave him an ovation by whistling over their radios. This helped relieve some of the tension flying combat missions. Pilot fatigue, same as combat fatigue, existed among the pilots. Our flight surgeons spent time sitting around in the ready rooms observing the pilots for excess fatigue. A major symptom was a change in a pilot's personality, e.g., a pilot might start a fight over a seemly minor incident. After a pilot reached his limit, he was grounded from flying, sent to medical sick bay, sedated with sleeping pills for three days of total rest.

At the end of each thirty day combat period, while en route to Yokosuka, the chaplains conducted memorial services for pilots and any ships personnel that had been lost on the previous combat tour on the line. The next night, squadrons and various ship division personnel put on a musical variety show with short comedy skits between acts. To provide a stage for the production, they lowered the ships forward elevator. There was no lack of talent and competition.

Just before Christmas, the toughest holiday to observe aboard ship, the variety show preparations had started. One of the jet squadrons had a petty officer who had experience in directing choral singing groups. He organized a choral group of pilots and enlisted men to sing Christmas songs and other songs in three-part harmony. They made choir robes out of old parachute material, and the singers wore their dark-blue uniform pants. Each row of singers held white electrically lit wands representing candles as they sang. There wasn't a dry eye in the audience, and the singers received many encores.

Three *AD* bomber pilots created a popular skit which was a pantomime of a *Spike Jones* hit song. They were creative with their various sound effects. One pilot held a string of beer cans to resemble chimes and hit them in time to the music. Another pilot looked really goofy with a pair of spring-loaded glasses with rotating eyeballs. All three of them, one a congressman's son, were later shot down and killed. A young, slightly built junior lieutenant ship's supply officer, who was a solo singer, wowed us with his deep booming voice while belting out some of the current popular songs.

The food served in the officer's mess was just plain lousy, and after all our complaining, this same young lieutenant was newly assigned to manage the mess. On his first day running the mess, he placed notes on each officer's plate and asked for suggestions to improve the food. He changed the menus and the quality of the food within a week. He raised everyone's morale with his wonderful singing and the great job he accomplished with his improvements to our mess.

One of the best R & R hotels was the famous and beautiful *Fujia Hotel* nestled up in the mountains with a wonderful view of the snow-peaked Mount Fuji. The hotel had numerous luxury hot baths, all with names like the *Neptune* and *Roman*. Reservations to the hotel were allocated to the squadrons, but there were never enough rooms available for all the pilots. Staff personnel of the military headquarters in Tokyo controlled the reservations, and I noticed some of the same group of Army staff officers at the hotel the two times I was lucky enough to have reservations. It was the same old story of the military — staff personnel always had the inside track on the goodies, and the combat troops got what was left.

Winter scene - Fujiya Hotel, Miyanoshita, Japan - Fisher photo

Sometimes, we'd ride bicycles from our R & R hotels along the rural countryside roads passing through small villages where older people would smile and wave, and small children would run behind us yelling and waving. You felt a little like *The Pied Piper*. Rural Japan was beautiful, and the people were extremely friendly.

The Army controlled the logistics for food in Japan. Because of that, the Navy seemed to receive the oldest cold-storage eggs. A fresh egg has a fairly rough shell; however, the shells on the eggs we were served were so smooth that you would have thought they had been *Simonized*. The cooked eggs had a sickly-green tint, which we smothered with catsup. Some of my last morning briefing statements to my pilots before leaving our ready room to man our aircraft was, "Go puke up the eggs and take your nervous pee."

KOREAN WAR

Our combat tour was coming to an end. The task-force admiral had directed that all of our targets for the last three days be close to the Korean coast and within easy rescue range for helos — good news for the pilots! On the last day on the line, my flight division drew the last late-afternoon mission. As my pilots were suiting up for the last squadron mission, pilots, who already had completed their flight missions and knew they were going home, paraded into the ready room wearing their clean khaki uniforms and grinning. That sight increased my determination that my pilots would also safely return home to their families. In my briefing session, I told them we could all salvo our bombs over the assigned target. Then the pilots looked at me incredulously but wearing big silly grins.

When we flew over the coastline south of Wonsan, my section leader noticed some boxcars along the railroad line which were in different positions than they were from the day before. He figured there was a camouflaged steam locomotive down there. He asked permission to drop out of formation with his wingman to search the area at a lower altitude. He found a locomotive covered with mud-covered tarps. Both pilots released their 1,000-pound bombs but had near misses on the target. As I dove down and lined my gun sight up on the locomotive, I fired my 20mm guns, and white steam blew out through the tattered tarps. We had a "live one." For the next half hour, we worked that locomotive over. The staff intelligence officers wouldn't give us credit for its destruction unless we rolled the locomotive on its side. That engine stayed upright because the large wheels had been blown off and it just kept settling deeper into the ground. We were picking up small-arms fire, and it wasn't worth the trouble to linger any longer. After flying out over Wonsan Bay, I ordered the pilots back into formation. Some of the pilots asked for permission to keep strafing so that our squadron's ordinance men wouldn't need to unload the guns. These pilots had agreed to salvo their bombs, but now they wanted to needlessly risk their necks some more. There's something about young Navy pilots when once strapped in their cockpits, they become fearless.

On the way back to the *Essex,* a couple of our crooners ignored radio discipline and composed a ditty to serenade the ship's Air Operations

Officer, whom they knew would be monitoring our tactical radio channel. In the spirit of the moment, he even egged them on. When we landed, we all felt exhilarated. We had flown our last mission and snagged a live locomotive to boot.

To convince myself that the *Essex* was really leaving the task force, I showered, got back in uniform, and then wandered up on the flight deck at dusk to watch the ship pull away from the task force and head for Yokosuka. Now I had ambivalent feelings of relief and sadness: relief I was going home and sadness for those pilots who would never return to their families.

It took a long seven days to reach Pearl Harbor from Japan. After the *Essex* docked at Ford Island at Pearl Harbor, I stood with some of our squadron pilots on the flight deck enjoying the balmy breezes. Aloha! When we finally departed from Pearl Harbor, it would take the *Essex* four more long days before she would be steaming into San Diego Bay.

CDR Fisher on flight deck of Essex as ship is being docked at Pearl Harbor - April 1952 - Personal photo

KOREAN WAR

After the *Essex* entered the San Diego Bay and the tugboats pushed the *Essex* close to the dock at NAS North Island, I spotted my red-headed daughter Susan, wearing a white sweater and standing in the front line of the large gathering of families and their friends. It's difficult to fully describe the emotional experience of being reunited with my family on the dock that day. My youngest daughter, Bobbie, held my hand tightly and wouldn't let go.

The next day, Bobbie and I walked to the barbershop. She sat and watched me getting a haircut, never taking her eyes off me. She had grown a lot in the eight months I'd been gone. During all of my combat missions, I carried back-to-back snapshots of Annie along with Susan and Bobbie each taking a turn holding our pet cat, "Snookie." Having these photos kept my family close to me. Additionally, we had heard that the Koreans were family orientated, and I felt a family photo might help if I were captured.

CHAPTER 23
DUTY ON THE BEACH

After being detached from the squadron, I was interviewed by the Personnel Director of ComAirPac. He said, "Clayton, I think you need a chance to see more of your family," so he assigned me to a billet in his Personnel Division. This assignment meant my family and I could remain in Coronado another year.

Checking Out in a Jet Fighter

A fighter pilot and shipmate from the *Hornet,* who had also survived the Battle of Santa Cruz, currently commanded a squadron of photo jet *Cougar F9Fs* based at NAS Miramar. He visited me in my office and told me, "Fisher, it's about time you checked out in one of my jets." So, I took him up on his offer and flew a *F9F* flight simulator to prepare myself. I practically memorized the pilot's handbook and was better prepared to check out in the jet aircraft, than any other plane I'd ever flown.

Finally, my big day arrived. The standard procedure for checking out in a single-seat jet is to have an experienced "chase pilot" assigned to take off in another fighter immediately behind your plane to monitor your flight. CDR "Zeke" Cormier, a former leader of the *Blue Angels,* was assigned as my chase pilot. After climbing into the cockpit, I carefully checked all the various switches and went over the take-off checklist. Satisfied, I started the engine, but Zeke quickly jumped up on my right wing and quickly changed some of the switches. While I was still trying to figure out which switches he had changed, he was already taxiing out to the main runway. As I gingerly followed him, still glancing at those switches, I was worried. Why had Zeke changed those switches?

Once in the air, and reaching about 300 feet, my cockpit began filling up with what appeared to be white smoke, coming from behind my seat. The worst thing that can happen to a pilot on his first flight in an unfamiliar aircraft is to face a serious emergency situation. After calling the control tower and declaring an emergency, I heard Zeke say, "Turn off your cabin pressurization switch." With the switch off, the white mist of carbon dioxide rapidly dissipated. It took me a little time to relax.

Completing my flight with no further problems, I then called the tower for permission to land. Due to the flight's short duration, the plane had not burned a lot of fuel; consequently, the plane would be heavy for my first landing. When the fuel is burned down in a jet fighter, it becomes very light for landings. Another big difference between propeller aircraft and jet aircraft is the landing approach. In a propeller aircraft, you normally pull up the nose a little to decrease your rate of descent, but in jets, if you pull the nose up to break the descent, it increases the rate of descent. In a jet, you add engine thrust, to slow your rate of decent. As I was almost ready to touch down, I reduced my throttle a little too soon and made a rather hard but solid landing. Anyway, my critics told me it was a great landing.

Officer-In-Charge of the Basic Instrument Training Unit-Pensacola

After a pleasant and happy year on the staff of ComAirPac, I received orders to the flight-training command at the naval air station at Pensacola, Florida, and was assigned as the Officer-in-Charge of the Basic Instrument Training Unit based at Corry Field. We called the flow of flight students in training "going through the pipeline." My responsibility was to keep the flow moving through the pipeline utilizing nearly 70 flight instructors. It was hard to believe the training unit flew the old WWII vintage *SNJs* with their obsolete old radios. Fortunately, the *SNJs* were soon replaced with new North American *T-28* equipped with the latest radio navigation and flight instrument equipment. It was the first brand-new Navy aircraft I ever flew. We called the *T-28* the "Cadillac" of the propeller aircraft. With its tricycle landing gear and excellent foreword visibility you could zip along the taxi strips to the runways, just like driving a car.

Commanding Officer Utility Squadron Three-Pacific Fleet

The two-year tour at Pensacola passed too swiftly, and I was then assigned as the commanding officer of Utility Squadron Three based at Ream Field Naval Air Facility in Imperial Beach, California. The squadron provided old *F6F Hellcat* fighters that had been converted to radio-controlled target drones for NAS Miramar-based jet fighters to practice firing their air-to-air missiles.

There were designated gunnery lanes at sea, south of the Coronado Islands which are southwest of Imperial Beach. The drone was controlled by another standard *F6F* fighter after being launched by ground-controllers. Conversely, the pilot flying the control fighter guided the drone back to the airfield, lined it up with a runway and turned control back to the Ground Controllers to land the drone. If a drone was too damaged to land or still flying uncontrolled creating and becoming a possible menace, the chase plane pilot had the fun of shooting the drone down.

Because I had logged a lot of flight time in the *F6F*, I was able to qualify as a drone-control pilot. The control plane flew formation on the drone and had special controls in it to fly the drone. You were simultaneously flying two planes. When you entered the gunnery lanes, you positioned the drone a few hundred yards abeam of your plane so to be well clear of the missiles fired at the drone.

Naval Air Station Miramar-San Diego

During my final tour and because retirement for the Navy was now looming ahead, Annie and I bought a lot in Coronado and built a nice home near the beach. I expected orders to a sea-duty billet and was surprised when I arrived one morning at the squadron to see a sign over my office door, "NAS Miramar." It was good and bad news;

good for my family, but bad for my future career. I needed a billet as a ship's officer for career reasons. Now the twilight of my naval career would be at NAS Miramar. There I served as the base Air Operations Officer and the Executive Officer. Due to a six-month delay of a new prospective commanding officer reporting for duty, I also served as the Commanding Officer. Being the commanding officer of this large master jet station, nicknamed "Fightertown USA," and later the home of the U.S. Navy Fighter Weapons School known as *Top Gun,* which became famous after the movie *Top Gun,* was a proud time in my aviation career.

One morning, during my assignment as the air operations officer of the air station, my secretary told me there was a Chief Petty Officer Ferguson in her office who asked to see me. The name Ferguson didn't register at first but when he walked into my office, Chief Ferguson was George Ferguson who had been my radioman and gunner during that fateful day on 27 October 1942 during the carrier battle of Santa Cruz, over sixteen years ago. What an exciting meeting, George was now the leading Senior Chief Petty Officer assigned to the staff of a carrier air group based at Miramar. We played hooky from our work, spending the next three afternoons in the Miramar Chief Petty Officers Club, reminiscing about our experiences during the battles of Midway and Santa Cruz and our various duty assignments.

I logged some flight hours in the air station's McDonnell *F2H-2* twin-engine fighter, so now I'd be able to tell my grandchildren, Grandpa was once a "jet jockey." On 13 February, 1961, I flew my last flight of my naval career in a twin-engine transport *R4D-5,* the Navy's upgraded version of the famous old WWII Douglas *DC-3* transport. With a co-pilot and crew chief, we took off on a beautiful clear starlit night and flew over Los Angeles and San Diego. It was a sad nostalgic moment for me after landing. I shook hands with my copilot and crew chief, and then kicked one of the plane's tires and thought to myself, "Fisher, you survived!" I would never pilot another Navy airplane again. I had a sneaking suspicion that I had used up all of my luck.

*My retirement ceremony - CDR Fisher and CAPT Bailey, NAS Miramar -
U.S. Navy photo*

On 1 March 1961, I retired after twenty-one years of naval service and
moved my family from government quarters back to our home in
Coronado. After adjusting to civilian life, I became a real-estate broker
and property developer. The successful development of fifty-one
commercial condominiums in Coronado, California became my swan
song in the business world and full retirement.

As they say goodbye in Japan, Sayonara.

CPSIA information can be obtained at www.ICGtesting.com
Printed in the USA
BVOW040011101011

273195BV00001B/1/P

9 781432 739119